The Mirabelle Cookbook

The Mirabelle Cookbook

Marco Pierre White

EBURY PRESS

First published in Great Britain in 1999

1 3 5 7 9 10 8 6 4 2

Ebury Press
Random House, 20 Vauxhall Bridge Road, London SW1V 2SA

Random House Australia Pty Limited
20 Alfred Street, Milsons Point, Sydney, New South Wales 2061, Australia

Random House New Zealand Limited
18 Poland Road, Glenfield, Auckland 10, New Zealand

Random House South Africa (Pty) Limited
Endulini, 5A Jubilee Road, Parktown 2193, South Africa

The Random House Group Limited Reg. No. 954009
www.randomhouse.co.uk

Papers used by Ebury Press are natural, recyclable products made from wood grown in sustainable forests.

A CIP catalogue record for this book is available from the British Library.

ISBN 0 09 186833 5

Design by David Fordham.
Photographs by William Lingwood
Typeset by MATS, Southend-on-Sea, Essex
Printed and bound in Italy by New Interlitho Italia S.p.a., Milan

CONTENTS

s

st

f

m

p

Mirabelle

LONDON

ℐNTRODUCTION

WHEN I ACQUIRED the Mirabelle restaurant in 1997 I felt rather as if I had found myself in charge of the crown jewels or a stately home. It was a restaurant with a world-famous name, suffused with history, now rather down on its luck, but still with that aura of glamour and prestige which no number of false new dawns and reopenings had quite removed.

Despite its famous name, it is not really all that old. It was founded shortly before World War II, in the basement of a not very distinguished 1930s block of flats in Curzon Street, Mayfair. It survived the war-time austerity, serving the better-off American servicemen stationed in London or diplomats working at the nearby embassy in Grosvenor Square, and reached its peak in the 1950s and 1960s, when such luminaries as Nubar Gulbenkian, Orson Welles, Aristotle Onassis, Rex Harrison, Laurence Olivier and Vivien Leigh were among its regular clientèle. Winston Churchill lunched there frequently, John-Paul Getty had a regular table in the corridor so he could watch the other guests pass by, and another table was always kept reserved in case of royal visitors. The head chef for over twenty-five years was Jean Drees, a Frenchman who made his career in London after the war, and by all accounts was a superlative cook of the old school.

But the glory years gradually faded, and the restaurant changed hands several times in the 1970s and 1980s. In 1991 it was acquired by a large Japanese corporation with wide international interests in the leisure industry, which set out to try and restore it to its former glory. They recruited a distinguished chef de cuisine, Michael Croft, brought back the former general manager, Victor Moruzzi, invested heavily in the design and décor, and restocked the cellars with a magnificent range of wines (more about this later). They also introduced a Japanese touch – two Teppanyaki grill rooms, offering this traditional food accompanied by authentic Japanese service.

OPPOSITE: Bousset's charming drawing graced the cover of the Mirabelle menu for nearly 30 years.

The timing may have been wrong – the early 1990s were a time of recession, particularly in the restaurant trade – and the venture was not the success its owners hoped for, so eventually they put it on the market once again. When I first visited the premises in 1997, I was struck not only by the huge potential of the site, but also by the sad evidence of gradual decline. I decided to have a go myself.

My aim was to bring this glamorous place into the modern age, making it much less élitist, and offering really good food at affordable prices. I embarked on a major revamp of the interior, completely redesigning the reception and bar areas, re-equipping the restaurant in a much cooler and more laid-back style, restoring the magnificent pine room, and making a real feature of the beautiful garden that lies at the back. I filled the walls with specially commissioned artwork and drawings and paintings from my own collection. And I designed a menu which would echo some of the history of the place while at the same time offering dishes that suit the modern taste. 'Affordable glamour' was my watchword.

But let me go back a little, and describe the setting of the Mirabelle. It is in the heart of London's Mayfair, which is today one of London most luxurious and exclusive residential areas, and where land is worth millions of pounds an acre. Set on the corner of Bolton Street and Curzon Street, it is just opposite two great London institutions, the hairdresser G. Trumper, and the bookseller Haywood Hill. Around the corner is Shepherd's Market, that charming little enclave which mixes low life with expensive small shops and cafés.

Mayfair's history goes back to 1280, when Edward I granted a licence for an annual week-long fair to take place here in May, in what was then largely open country, and from which he drew revenue. The fair flourished over the centuries, eventually becoming a cattle market – which annoyed some of the noble owners of grand houses round about, but pleased the monarchy a stone's throw away in St James's Palace.

In the 18th century, development of this whole area began in earnest. The land was owned by two noble families, the Grosvenors and the Berkeleys – hence Grosvenor Square to the north, and Berkeley Square to the east. But much of the practical architecture and design of this development was carried out for them by one Edward Shepherd, whose partner was Nathaniel Curzon. Shepherd also built for himself the large and imposing white house on the north side of Curzon Street which was subsequently sold to the Marquess of Crewe, and renamed Crewe House.

The market which bears his name was developed for stallholders to open all the year round, not just in May – tiny shops selling goods of all sorts to rich visitors

OPPOSITE: *Mayfair in the 1760s: the whole area was developed by two noble families, the Grosvenors and the Berkeleys. Shepherd's Market and Curzon Street were just south of the 28-acre Hay Hill Farm, which only 15 years earlier had been open land.*

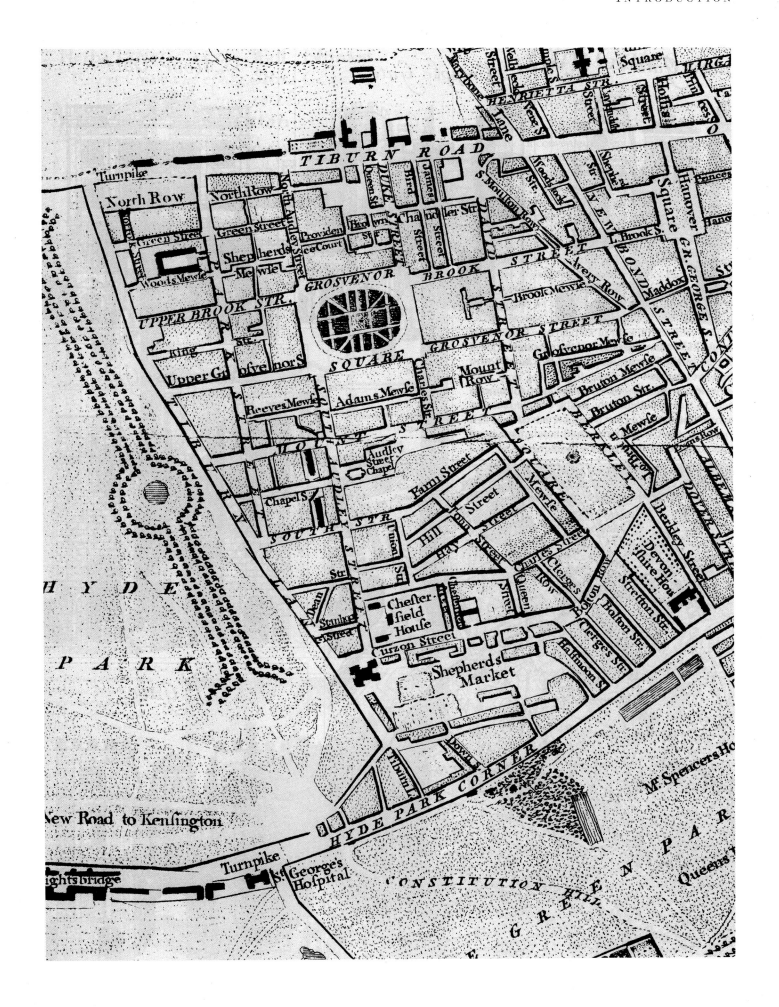

and passers-by – much as it is today. To walk round it now is to take a journey into the past.

To give you a sense of what this whole area was like in the 18th century, I have reproduced a contemporary map, published in 1761. It shows the two great estates, the Grosvenors and Berkeleys, alongside one another. The founder of the Grosvenor estate – a hundred acres of Mayfair – was the child heiress Mary Davies; and she might easily have acquired the rest of Mayfair too if she had married the 5th Lord Berkeley of Stratton, to whom she was engaged at the age of seven. Instead, she married Sir Thomas Grosvenor in 1677, when she was twelve, and it was their son Richard who built up the area. Lord Berkeley built his square and surrounding streets a few years later, and the 28-acre farm on which he built it is commemorated in several street names, like Hay Hill and Farm Street.

*   *   *

One idea that occurred to me when planning to reopen the Mirabelle was to see what could be learned by looking at the cooking that had been done there in the past, and possibly reconstructing or reproducing some of the classic dishes for which the restaurant had been renowned. But it was not easy to find them. The nearest I could get was from a book called *Cuisine Mirabelle*, published twenty years ago, which included a number of recipes taken down by the authors from the chef Jean Drees. It is quite instructive, to my mind, to compare the elaborate food that was taken for granted in high-class restaurants in those days with what we serve our customers now.

I have taken as an example the recipe for *Cotelettes d'agneau Prince de Galles*, partly because it illustrates the difference, and partly because it is typical of the style of cooking. The recipe's origins go back much further than the life of the Mirabelle, because it was created by Maxim's in Paris (with which the Mirabelle had a long connection) in the 1890s for the future king Edward VII. Here it is:

Take 3 thin cutlets per person. Trim any unwanted fat but do not overdo it. Make a spread by mincing $\frac{1}{2}$ pound of veal and mixing it with a purée of mushroom, tarragon, seasoning, 1 or 2 dessertspoons of brandy and about $\frac{1}{2}$ cup of double cream. You should have a stiff consistency which you now spread on both sides of the cutlets. Crumb them if you wish, though this is not absolutely necessary. Sauté the 'stuffed' cutlets in butter for 5–6 minutes each side. Sauté some thinly-sliced raw potatoes (these can be done in

GENERAL ELECTION NIGHT
26th MAY, 1955

MIRABELLE
56, Curzon Street, Mayfair, W.1.

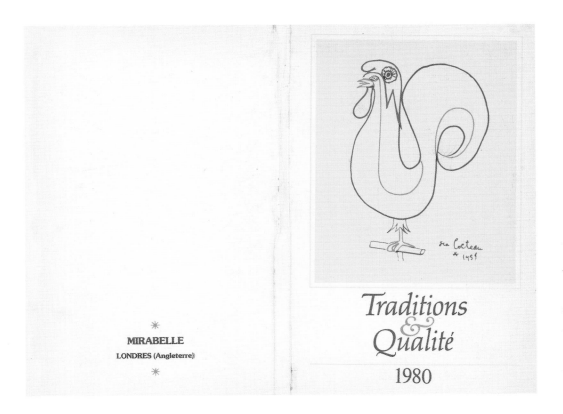

MIRABELLE
LONDRES (Angleterre)

Traditions & Qualité 1980

The Mirabelle was one of only two British restaurants to be included in 1980 in the Traditions et Qualité *selection of best international restaurants (the other was the Gavroche). But by then the Mirabelle was probably past its best. The drawing is by Jean Cocteau (1959).*

another pan coincidentally) and spread them on a dish. Lay the cooked cutlets on top, garnish them with button mushrooms and artichoke hearts warmed in butter, and cover with either a madeira or périgourdine sauce, both of which may readily be bought.

For one thing, the recipe is much less explicit about details than I have tried to be in this book. The 'spread' of minced veal and puréed mushrooms is obviously crucial, but very little guidance is offered as to how to ensure it has the 'stiff consistency' necessary to make it adhere to the cutlets. And of course it doesn't tell you how to make a madeira or périgourdine sauce, but just tells you to go out and buy them.

In case you are interested, this is how to make a Périgueux sauce: you need 50 g (2 oz) unsalted butter, two thinly sliced shallots, 125 g (4$\frac{1}{2}$ oz) thinly sliced button mushrooms, 600 ml (21 fl oz) veal stock, a glass of white wine, 100 g (4 oz) fresh truffles peeled and cut into small dice, and seasoning. Sweat the shallots and mushrooms in half the butter, add the veal stock and reduce over a low heat for an hour or so. In the rest of the butter, sweat the diced truffles. Put them into the hot sauce, stir and season. Cover the pan and let the ingredients infuse for a while before serving. You can substitute Madeira for the wine, to get that additional flavour which brings out the taste of the truffles.

When looking over the old menus, some of which go back to the 1950s, it is interesting to see how little things changed over two decades – apart, that is, from the prices. The hors d'oeuvres comprised caviar (which cost 22s 6d for an ounce in 1955 and £15.00 in the 1970s); snails à la bourguignonne, lobster cocktail, avocado with crab, York or Bayonne ham, a chef's pâté, smoked trout, potted

In 1980 a dinner was held at the Mirabelle to celebrate its long links with Maxim's in Paris, with food prepared by the Maxim's chefs, Alex Humbert and Louis Barthe. The dining room was elaborately decorated, and so was the food (see page 13, opposite).

shrimps, and that postwar delicacy the grapefruit (presumably with a glacé cherry in the middle). The range of fish was also very limited by today's standards: just sole, trout, turbot, red mullet, salmon and lobster. For more than twenty years the restaurant served a Polish borscht which it called 'Barszcz à la Cracovienne'.

The recipes I have included here are generally much more accessible to the home cook than some of those I have published in previous books, which reflects the fact that restaurant food these days is becoming simpler. If you wanted to pick just the simplest dishes here, you could choose from the following:

Soups: Tomato Consommé
Starters: Smoked Salmon Properly Garnished or Salad Lyonnaise
Fish Dishes: Grilled Lemon Sole with Tartare Sauce or Cod and Chips
Meat Dishes: Bang Bang Chicken or Cottage Pie with Pea Purée or Steak and Eggs with HP Sauce
Puddings: Raspberries in Pink Champagne Jelly or Tiramisù

All of these can be cooked at home with no difficulty, can be done in minutes rather than hours, and don't require elaborate or specialised equipment. But my aim is to encourage you, as you gain confidence, to move on from these to the slightly more complicated recipes which really do repay the extra effort. I am very well aware that we professional chefs have great advantages over the home cook. We have pairs of hands to help with all the chopping and preparation; we have ovens and stoves that are permanently on and consistently hot; we have more money to spend and easier access to really good ingredients. But you should not be deterred by this. The standard of cooking in British homes has improved beyond all recognition over the last few years, as people have discovered really

good food in restaurants here and abroad, and sought to reproduce it at home. Recipe books like this one provide access to the skills and methods of the professional cook, and the only way to learn is by doing it – and doing it again and again until you have perfected it.

There are of course lots of short cuts you can take. I recommend that you make your own stocks for soups and sauces, but that is certainly a very time-consuming business, and it is possible now to buy perfectly decent stock even from the supermarkets, which can be kept in the freezer until needed. You needn't garnish your dishes as elaborately as we sometimes do – and indeed to my mind the more simply a dish is presented the better. There is a tradition in British restaurants of serving every main course with an excessive panoply of vegetables and garnishes. This is never done in France, where the food culture is more deeply rooted. There, a chef can present a simple sea bream with a red wine sauce, or salmon with a sorrel sauce, without cluttering the plate with additions. Over the last few years in all my restaurants I have sought to simplify my presentation, cutting through to the essentials – and you can do this at home just as well.

ABOVE: A ham in pastry.

BELOW: An elaborately decorative cold lobster dish.

13

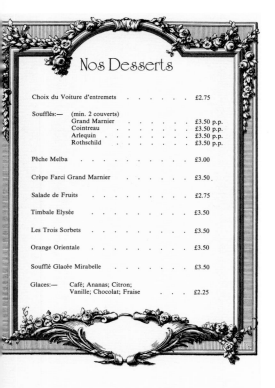

Nos Desserts

Choix du Voiture d'entremets	. . . . .	£2.75
Soufflés:— (min. 2 couverts)		
Grand Marnier	. . . . .	£3.50 p.p.
Cointreau	. . . . .	£3.50 p.p.
Arlequin	. . . . .	£3.50 p.p.
Rothschild	. . . . .	£3.50 p.p.
Pêche Melba	. . . . . .	£3.00
Crèpe Farci Grand Marnier	. . . .	£3.50
Salade de Fruits	. . . . . .	£2.75
Timbale Elysée	. . . . .	£3.50
Les Trois Sorbets	. . . . .	£3.50
Orange Orientale	. . . . .	£3.50
Soufflé Glacée Mirabelle	. . . .	£3.50
Glaces:— Café; Ananas; Citron;		
Vanille; Chocolat; Fraise	. . .	£2.25

ABOVE: A pudding menu from the 1970s.

BELOW: A rich cake from the same period.

I mentioned earlier that there was something rather special about the Mirabelle's wine cellar, and I thought it might interest readers who are 'into' wine as much as food to know a bit about it. The various owners of the restaurant since its foundation more than sixty years ago have always ensured that there was a decent and broad-ranging cellar, which is a prerequisite for any establishment with pretensions to serve the best. But when the Japanese company acquired the Mirabelle in 1991 they made a decision to invest really seriously in the wine, and the result is a cellar which I think is one of the most notable of its kind in the country.

It is so extensive that we have to break it down into two. The day-to-day cellar is listed in the menu, and comprises over 300 different wines of recent growth, ready for drinking now, with selections from all the fine wine-growing areas of the world. The most expensive is the 1989 Penfold Grange Bin 95, from South Australia, currently at £515 a bottle, but there are plenty of reasonably priced wines there too.

But the fine wine list is truly extraordinary. Let me just give a few examples. The range of Penfold Grange Bin 95 (probably the best wine currently made in Australia) includes the 1964, 1967, 1968, 1969, 1970, 1972, 1973, 1974, and 1976, and then every year up to 1991. The clarets include all the first growths, beginning with magnums of Latour and Lafite from 1861 and 1874, and running right through the decades to the 1990s. There are 1989 methuselahs (the contents of eight standard bottles) of all six of the major wines from Romanée Conti, including La Tache, Richebourg and Grand Echézeaux. There are superb champagnes, including the rare 1961 Dom Pérignon and Krug and the magnificent 1975 Cristal Roederer. If you ever visit the Mirabelle, and are a wine buff, ask to see this list. It will amaze you.

In the Mirabelle's surviving archives – and with so many changes of ownership in recent years, these are rather scant – I discovered, as I have said, a number of menus covering the years from the 1950s on, which you will find reproduced towards the back of this book. To anyone interested in changing tastes in restaurant food over the last half century these are revealing, as are the escalating prices for the same dishes. I have also included the Mirabelle's current menu, for comparison's sake.

The people who make the Mirabelle what it is today are, of course, the staff who work there, a group of very dedicated people who maintain the standards this kind of restaurant requires. I am not the Mirabelle's chef. This role is shared between three highly talented young men, and they and their supporting kitchen staff are listed below:

Cotelettes d'agneau Prince de Galles, a good example of the classical Mirabelle cuisine of the 1950s, though its origins go back much further: it was created by Maxim's in the 1890s for the future king Edward VII.

EXECUTIVE HEAD CHEF
Charlie Rushton

HEAD CHEF
Spencer Patrick

PASTRY CHEF
Anthony M. Richards

SOUS-CHEFS
Tony Joseph   Sean McDonald

Juan Connesso   Michael O'Connor
Wi-Anne Fick   Marcus Ree-Taylor
Justin Flodman   Vanessa Rego
Vaughan Keenan   Curtis Stone
Brian McGann   Richard Wimbleton
James Metcalfe

And the front-of-house staff are as follows:

GENERAL MANAGER
Frédéric Serol

RESTAURANT MANAGER
Christophe Capron

CHIEF SOMMELIER
Claude Douard

HOST
Louis Emmanuelli

SPECIAL PERSONAL ASSISTANT TO MARCO PIERRE WHITE
Takanori Ishii

HEAD RECEPTIONIST
Marion Brown

Marco Pierre White
August 1999

S

SOUPS

S

gazpacho

S

gazpacho

SERVES 4

700 g (1 lb 9 oz) plum tomatoes, skinned and de-seeded
½ cucumber, peeled and seeded
½ onion, chopped
3 garlic cloves, chopped
5 red peppers, seeded and chopped
75 ml (3 fl oz) sherry vinegar
salt and freshly ground black pepper
Tabasco
2 tablespoons mayonnaise (Basic 15)

Liquidise the first six ingredients together, pass through a fine sieve, and season with salt and pepper and a little Tabasco. Serve chilled.

Gazpacho is delicious on its own, or sprinkled with croûtons, but at the Mirabelle we often add other ingredients. In the photograph, the soup contains langoustine tails, and a dollop of bright green mousse made from courgettes — but this is the kind of elaboration that really only restaurants, with all their pairs of hands, can manage.

S

Cream of celery soup

SERVES 4

250 g (9 oz) celery, finely sliced
250 g (9 oz) celeriac, peeled and finely sliced
1 onion, peeled and finely sliced
1 white part of leek, finely sliced
50 g (2 oz) unsalted butter
salt and freshly ground white pepper
100 g (4 oz) potatoes, peeled and finely sliced
500 ml (17½ fl oz) double cream
500 ml (17½ fl oz) chicken stock (Basic 1)
4 eggs
white wine vinegar
finely chopped chives

1. Sweat the celery, celeriac, onion and leek in the butter without colouring, until all the moisture has evaporated. Season with salt and pepper.
2. Place the raw potato slices in a pan with the cream and stock, bring to the boil, and pour over the rest of the vegetables. Cook on a high heat for 10 minutes, then liquidise and pass the soup through a sieve.
3. Bring a small pan of water to the boil, add a teaspoon of white wine vinegar, poach the eggs, and keep warm (for more detailed instructions, see the recipe for Poached Eggs Benedict, page 38).
4. To serve, place a poached egg in each soup bowl, pour the hot soup over, and sprinkle chopped chives on top.

truffled cabbage soup

SERVES 4

This sounds more difficult to make than it actually is – and the taste is absolutely superb!

8 dark green Savoy cabbage leaves
200 g (8 oz) spinach leaves
1 litre (33 fl oz) chicken stock (Basic 1)
150 g (5 oz) chopped smoked bacon
75 ml (3 fl oz) double cream
salt and freshly ground black pepper
1 tablespoon truffle oil
4 slices foie gras
12 sprigs flat-leaf parsley

1. Bring a large pan of salted water to the boil. Add the cabbage leaves, and after 5 minutes the spinach, and cook until tender (another 2 or 3 minutes). Drain, and blend in the liquidiser into a purée.
2. Place the chicken stock and smoked bacon in a pan and reduce by three quarters (to 250 ml (9 fl oz)). Then add the double cream and reduce further. Sieve to remove the bacon.
3. Bring the cream mixture back to the boil, and add the truffle oil and the cabbage purée. The colour should now be rich green. Blitz with a blender.
4. Heat a non-stick pan until very hot, and sear the foie gras slices quickly on both sides.
5. Pour the soup into bowls. Top each bowl with a slice of foie gras, and garnish with 3 sprigs of flat-leaf parsley and a little truffle oil.

cream of celery soup

truffled parsley soup with poached egg

truffled parsley soup with poached egg

SERVES 4

This soup can be served and enjoyed all the year round. Truffle oil is slightly less expensive than truffles themselves, but adds its unique flavour.

50 g (2 oz) parsley

200 g (8 oz) fresh spinach leaves, washed

1 litre (33 fl oz) chicken stock (Basic 1)

150 g (5 oz) smoked bacon, sliced

750 ml (26½ fl oz) double cream

salt and freshly ground black pepper

1 tablespoon truffle oil

4 eggs, poached

12 sprigs flat-leaf parsley

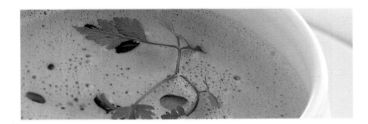

1. Bring a large pan of salted water to the boil. Add the parsley and after 3 minutes the spinach, and cook for another 3 minutes until tender. Drain, and blend to a purée in a liquidiser. Pass the purée through a fine sieve, and chill in the fridge.

2. Put the chicken stock and smoked bacon into a pan and reduce by three quarters (to 250 ml (9 fl oz)). Then add the double cream and reduce further. Sieve to remove the bacon.

3. Bring the cream mixture back to the boil, and add the truffle oil and the parsley purée. The colour should be rich green.

4. Bring a small pan of water to the boil, add a teaspoon of white wine vinegar, poach the eggs, and keep warm (for more detailed instructions, see the recipe for Poached Eggs Benedict, page 38).

5. Place a poached egg in each soup bowl, pour the soup over, and garnish each with three sprigs of flat-leaf parsley and a little truffle oil.

garbanzo (chick pea broth)

SERVES 4

250 g (9 oz) dried chick peas

½ teaspoon bicarbonate of soda

1.7 litres (5¼ pints) warm water

1 small onion, chopped

1 large tomato, chopped

1 green pepper, cored, seeded and chopped

1 head garlic

2 chicken stock cubes, crumbled

50 ml (2 fl oz) olive oil

250 g (9 oz) string beans, each cut into 3 pieces

450 g (1 lb) pumpkin

2 medium potatoes, peeled and chopped

2 bunches spinach, washed and chopped

freshly ground salt

1. Soak the chick peas overnight with the bicarbonate of soda in warm water.

2. Rinse and drain. Put the chick peas in a large flameproof casserole dish and add the onion, tomato, pepper, garlic, stock cubes and oil. Cook over a medium heat for 2½ to 3 hours, stirring occasionally. Check the broth after 1½ hours, and add more boiling water if necessary – not cold water, which will harden the chick peas. For the same reason, don't remove the pan from the heat during cooking.

3. When the chick peas are cooked, stir in the string beans, pumpkin and potatoes and cook for a further 15 to 20 minutes until the potatoes are nearly soft. Add the spinach leaves and heat through for another few minutes.

4. Season to taste, ladle into warm soup plates, and serve with crusty bread.

S

tomato consommé

SERVES 4

This is a perfect soup for a hot summer's day, light and full of flavour.

2 tablespoons tomato purée

6 beefsteak tomatoes

3 regular tomatoes

4 stalks celery

4 stalks each chervil, chives, tarragon and parsley

1 teaspoon cracked white peppercorns

large pinch sea salt

FOR THE GARNISH

batons of chives

4 regular tomatoes, peeled, seeded and diced

½ cucumber, scooped into small balls

chervil leaves

1. Blitz together all the ingredients except the garnish in a liquidiser. Tip into a bowl, and leave to marinate for 6 hours.

2. Strain the soup through a colander lined with muslin, and leave the consommé to drain through slowly. Chill until ready to serve.

3. To serve, divide the consommé among the four soup bowls, and garnish with chive batons, diced tomatoes, cucumber balls and chervil leaves.

Cappuccino of mushrooms

SERVES 4

This soup is very popular at the Mirabelle. We give it an extra zip by sprinkling dried ceps or morelles, blitzed to a powder, on top of it just before serving.

1 small onion, peeled and sliced

1 white part of leek, sliced

50 g (2 oz) unsalted butter

500 g (1 lb 1 oz) white button mushrooms, sliced

1 litre (33 fl oz) chicken stock (Basic 1)

500 ml (17½ fl oz) double cream

100 g (4 oz) potatoes, peeled and sliced

salt and freshly ground white pepper

chervil sprigs

1. Sweat the onion and leek in the butter over a low heat without colouring, then add the mushrooms. Continue cooking until all the moisture has evaporated, still without colouring.

2. Place the chicken stock, cream and raw potato slices in a pan and bring to the boil. Pour this over the vegetables, and cook on a medium heat for 10 minutes.

3. Liquidise the soup and strain it through a sieve. If it is slightly too thick, add a little more chicken stock. Season.

4. To serve, heat the soup until just short of boiling, then froth it with a hand blender for 2 minutes to get the cappuccino effect. Pour into bowls, and sprinkle a little chervil over each.

Soupe au pistou de saint-jacques

SERVES 6

The base of this soup – the vegetables and stock etc – can be prepared in advance and reheated briefly at the last moment. The pistou can also be made in advance and chilled. Don't add the pistou and scallops until the very end.

30 g (1¼ oz) each of onion, carrot, celeriac, turnip, swede, potato,
green beans and courgette, cut into small dice
olive oil
1 litre (33 fl oz) fish stock (Basic 5)
salt and freshly ground white pepper
6 scallops, shelled and cleaned
court bouillon to cover (Basic 6)
100 g (4 oz) spaghetti
6 tablespoons pistou (Basic 19)

1. Sweat the onion in a little olive oil in a saucepan, then add the carrot and celeriac. After a few minutes add the turnip, swede and potato and sweat for a few minutes more. Add the beans and courgette at the end.
2. In a separate pan, bring the fish stock to the boil and pour over the vegetables. Bring back to the boil, then remove from the heat and season to taste.
3. Meanwhile, wash the scallops briefly and pat dry on kitchen paper. Cut the nuggets of white meat into three slices horizontally. Poach them for 1 minute only in the court bouillon with a little olive oil added. Drain.
4. Break the spaghetti into 2.5 cm (1 in) lengths and blanch in boiling salted water. Drain well, and add to the vegetable soup.
5. To serve, divide the hot soup between 6 soup bowls and add 1 tablespoon of pistou to each. Stir to emulsify, then drop 3 slices of poached scallop into each.

S

mussel and saffron soup

SERVES 4

The best way to clean mussels thoroughly is to put them in a bucket in the sink and run the cold tap over them for as long as possible (we do it for 6 hours). The moving water helps get all the grit and sand out of them. You should also knock off any barnacles with a knife, and tug off the 'beard' – the tuft that protrudes from the hinge.

At the Mirabelle we garnish this soup with diced potato and chives. Another idea might be croûtons. And it can be decorated with additional strands of saffron.

2 kg (4 lb 8 oz) mussels
1 onion, peeled and finely chopped
1 celery stalk, finely chopped
1 white part of leek, finely chopped
25 g (1 oz) unsalted butter
1 teaspoon curry powder
pinch saffron strands
½ teaspoon cayenne pepper
1 sprig thyme
1 bay leaf
600 ml (21 fl oz) white wine
300 ml (10½ fl oz) fish stock (Basic 5)
450 ml (16 fl oz) double cream
salt

1. Wash the mussels, pull off their beards, and wash them again carefully.
2. Sweat the vegetables gently in the butter for 5 minutes. Add the curry powder and saffron, cayenne and herbs, and then the mussels, and continue cooking gently, with the lid on, for another minute. Add the wine and stock, and cook for another few minutes until the mussels open.

3. Pick the mussels out, discarding any that have failed to open, and strain the stock through muslin or a fine sieve.
4. In a clean pan, reduce the stock by half. Add the cream, and reduce further until you have a coating consistency. Season with a little salt if required.
5. To serve, remove the mussels from their shells (making sure there are no beards), and place a few in each soup bowl. Heat the soup to just below boiling point, and pour over the mussels.

mussel and saffron soup

S

Vichyssoise with smoked haddock

Serves 4

750 g (1¾ lb) leeks (mainly white), finely sliced

350 g (12 oz) onions, peeled and finely sliced

100 g (4 oz) unsalted butter

350 g (12 oz) potatoes, peeled and finely sliced

900 ml (1½ pints) chicken stock (Basic 1), boiling

900 ml (1½ pints) water, boiling

200 ml (7 fl oz) double cream

salt and freshly ground white pepper

175 g (6 oz) smoked haddock fillets

300 ml (10 fl oz) milk and water, mixed

chopped chives

1. Sweat the leek and onion in the butter until they are soft, but without colouring. Then add the finely sliced raw potato, the boiling stock and water, and cook over a fast heat for 10 minutes.

2. Add the cream, and cook for a further 2 minutes. Liquidise, then pass through a fine sieve. Season to taste.

3. Poach the haddock in the milk and water for a few minutes, then drain and flake into large pieces.

4. To serve, put the sieved soup and chives into bowls, and divide the haddock flakes between them. Serve immediately.

st

Starters

fresh asparagus with sauce mousseline

st

fresh asparagus with sauce mousseline

SERVES 4

This is the perfect starter for a warm summer's day. English asparagus – the best in the world – is in season in May and June, which means it is a lot cheaper than when it has to be flown in from abroad. Cook and eat it as soon as possible after you buy it.

24 asparagus
salt and freshly ground black pepper
a little olive oil
fresh chervil to garnish
sauce mousseline (Basic 12)

1. Cut off the bottoms of the asparagus, and peel away 5 cm (2 in) of the skin from the bottom up. Blanch in boiling salted water for 4 to 6 minutes (depending on the size of the asparagus) until *al dente* (still slightly crisp).
2. Drain, brush with a little olive oil, and set 6 asparagus on warm plates. Serve with the sauce mousseline, garnished with fresh chervil.

pimientos asados

SERVES 4

4 large red peppers
4 large green peppers
3 large tomatoes
1 small-to-medium onion
1 teaspoon salt
1½ tablespoons white wine vinegar
4 tablespoons olive oil

1. Preheat the grill to low, and cook the peppers and tomatoes until they start to blister and blacken – about 30 minutes. Turn them occasionally. Leave to cool, and retain the juices.
2. Peel the cooked peppers and cut into thin strips. Peel the tomatoes, and chop.
3. Place the peppers and tomato in a large dish.
4. Peel and chop the onion very finely, and add to the salad. Sprinkle with salt, drizzle with oil and vinegar, and mix well. Cover and chill until ready to serve.

This salad can be served as individual portions, as we do it at the Mirabelle, or in a large bowl in the middle of the table to accompany a main course like sea bass.

Salad lyonnaise

SERVES 4

This is quick and simple to cook, a lovely and light spring salad, and makes a perfect starter. Frisée (or curly endive) looks just like a large, open, crinkly lettuce, but it is actually a member of the chicory family, and has quite a strong flavour.

2 heads curly endive (frisée)

100 ml (3½ fl oz) olive oil

20 croûtons made from a small, thinly-sliced baguette

45 ml (1¾ fl oz) white wine vinegar

salt and freshly ground black pepper

100 g (4 oz) bacon lardons

1 teaspoon vegetable oil

4 poached eggs (see the recipe for Poached Eggs Benedict, page 38)

10 g (¼ oz) chive batons

20 small sprigs chervil

1. Pick the yellow leaves off the endive, and discard the green. Wash thoroughly in cold water twice, leave to drain in a colander, and then spin lightly in a salad spinner. Keep in the fridge.

2. Heat 5 tablespoons of the olive oil in a pan and fry the croûtons until golden brown all over. Drain them on kitchen paper to get rid of excess oil.

3. Make a vinaigrette by mixing the rest of the olive oil and the vinegar together, and season.

4. Put the lardons in a pan, cover with water and bring to the boil. Then drain, and fry them in the vegetable oil until crisp. Keep warm.

5. Reheat the poached eggs in simmering seasoned water.

6. Mix the endive with the chives, and season. Toss in the vinaigrette, and the croûtons and lardons, and mix evenly.

7. Remove the eggs from the water, drain and season them, and put them on top of the salad with a little vinaigrette. Garnish with chervil and serve.

salad lyonnaise

quiche of leeks and gruyère

quiche of leeks and gruyère

SERVES 8

This rich, deep quiche has a brilliant creamy texture. Gruyère is a famous Swiss cheese made from unpasteurised cow's milk, firm and close-textured with a sprinkling of small holes. I like to serve the quiche with a simple salad of leaves tossed in a light dressing.

450 g (1 lb) puff pastry (Basic 28)

6 whole leeks

100 g (4 oz) unsalted butter

10 eggs

500 ml (17½ fl oz) milk

500 ml (17½ fl oz) double cream

salt and freshly ground black pepper

100 g (4 oz) Gruyère cheese, grated

You can adapt this recipe, using

mushrooms – morels or button

mushrooms – instead of leeks. Simply

sauté the mushrooms and add them to the

quiche mixture.

1. Preheat the oven to 180°C/350°F/Gas 4. Roll out the puff pastry so it is about 2½ mm (less than ⅛ in) thick and will line a 25 x 8 cm (10 x 3¼ in) pastry ring. Butter the ring, line it with greaseproof paper, and fill it with dry baking beans or lentils. Bake the pastry with the beans for about 20 minutes, then remove the beans and cook a little longer until the pastry is crisp.

2. Finely chop the leeks, washing and draining them thoroughly. Sweat them in the butter until they are tender and cooked, then drain well.

3. Mix together the eggs, milk and cream, season, and pass through a sieve.

4. Reduce the oven heat to 130°C/250°F/Gas ¾. Mix the cooked leeks with three-quarters of the cheese, and fill the pastry ring with the mixture. Cover with the egg mixture, and sprinkle the remaining cheese on top. Cook in the oven for 50 minutes.

5. Leave the quiche to stand for a while before removing the ring. Serve warm with a little salad.

Poached eggs benedict with hollandaise sauce

SERVES 4

This delicious dish is so rich that there is no need to butter the muffins. The ham should be a dry-cured, smoky one like Bayonne or Toulouse. The muffins can be bought.

st

8 eggs
½ litre (17½ fl oz) white wine vinegar
8 slices ham
4 English muffins
watercress to garnish
4 portions Hollandaise sauce (Basic 10)

1. Poach the eggs as follows. Fill a tall pan three-quarters with water, add the white wine vinegar, and bring the temperature up to 100°C/240°F. Turn down the flame. Break the eggs into the pan. After a few minutes remove them, and refresh in iced water. Trim the egg whites neatly with a knife, and reheat in hot salted water just before serving.
2. Turn on the grill to hot. Cut the ham to the approximate size of the muffins. Split and toast the muffins on both sides, and put a slice of ham on each. Put them under the grill to heat.
3. Place two muffin halves on each plate, with a hot, drained, poached egg on top, and spoon the Hollandaise sauce over them. Garnish with watercress and serve.

Tortilla de patatas (spanish omelette)

SERVES 4

5 medium potatoes weighing about 1.2 kg (3 lb)
1 large onion
1 teaspoon salt
vegetable oil for frying
6 large eggs

Tortillas can be served hot or cold, but I prefer mine cold. They are nicest about an hour after they've been made.

1. Peel the potatoes and onion and chop them into smallish, thinnish squares. Season with the salt.
2. Heat a large deep fat fryer until the oil is hot, add the potatoes and onion, and cook until they are soft and slightly golden. Drain, and place the vegetables in a bowl.
3. In another bowl beat the eggs, add them to the vegetables, which they should cover (if not, add another egg).
4. Place a large non-stick frying pan (about 25 cm (10 in) in diameter) on a medium heat with a little vegetable oil.

When it is hot, pour in the tortilla mixture. Flatten the top with a wooden spoon to spread the mixture, and cook gently for 5 to 10 minutes.
5. When the tortilla is set on the bottom, put a large heat-proof plate over the top of the frying pan, turn the tortilla over, and slide it back into the pan to cook the other side – for another 5 to 10 minutes.
6. When both sides are golden and the inside is firm but not hard, slide on to a large serving plate and allow the tortilla to cool a little.

poached eggs benedict with hollandaise sauce

smoked salmon properly garnished

Smoked salmon properly garnished

SERVES 4

st

The best smoked salmon has moist, glistening flesh, and is rosy pink with a faint hint of orange. The stronger cures tend to come from Scotland, made with Atlantic salmon caught there; but Irish and English cures can also be delicately flavoured. This dish is a classic starter – lemon juice is traditional because it cuts through the flavour and brings out the richness of the salmon – and this is how we present it at the Mirabelle.

500 g (1 lb 1 oz) sliced smoked salmon
black pepper
50 g (2 oz) shallots, finely chopped
20 g (¾ oz) flat-leaf parsley, cut into thin strips
50 g (2 oz) baby capers
50 g (2 oz) gherkins, chopped
2 hard-boiled eggs, grated
2 lemons, halved, and wrapped in muslin
100 g (4 oz) horseradish sauce
30 ml (1½ fl oz) double cream
cayenne pepper
the juice of half a lemon
4 slices of buttered brown bread

1. Divide the salmon equally between the four plates. Then grind a little black pepper over them.

2. Place the shallots, parsley, capers, gherkins and eggs in five separate piles on the edge of the smoked salmon, and put the lemons in the middle.

3. Make the horseradish cream by mixing together the horseradish sauce, cream, cayenne and lemon juice, and serve it in a little jug on the side, with the buttered brown bread.

You can buy horseradish sauce, or make it yourself from fresh or dried horseradish root. Bought sauce can be surprisingly variable in strength.

roulade of smoked salmon mirabelle

SERVES 4

15 g (½ oz) shallots, finely chopped
¼ teaspoon chopped garlic
15 g (½ oz) chives, finely chopped
pinch parsley, finely chopped
pinch salt
250 g (9 oz) fromage blanc, hung in muslin for 24 hours
100 g (4 oz) double cream, whipped to a soft peak
500 g (1 lb 1 oz) long strips of sliced smoked salmon

1. Fold the shallots, garlic, chives and parsley (together with a pinch of salt) into the fromage blanc. Then fold in the whipped double cream. Allow to set in the fridge for 2 to 3 hours.

2. Place the smoked salmon between two pieces of clingfilm and give it a light pressing with a rolling pin until it is 1 to 2 mm (¹⁄₁₆ in) thick. Remove the top clingfilm.

3. Place the fromage mixture in a piping bag, and pipe a strip along the leading edge of the smoked salmon. Then roll the salmon until you have a perfect cylinder. Keep it in the clingfilm, and tighten the ends with a little knot. Place in the fridge to set for 24 hours.

4. Remove the clingfilm, and with a very sharp knife cut the roulade on the diagonal into 7.5 mm (3 in) lengths. Serve two per person, with a little salad.

roulade of smoked salmon mirabelle

blinis with caviar and fromage blanc

SERVES 4

The blini mixture has to be made in advance. I use fresh yeast, which can be bought from the bakery section of most supermarkets. Instead of caviar you can use lumpfish roe or keta, which are of course much cheaper, but the effect won't be quite the same. We also serve these blinis with smoked salmon in place of the caviar (see page 46). You'll need about 400 g (14 oz) of smoked salmon. Put a portion on top of each blini, then a neat quenelle of fromage blanc, plus the caviar and chervil garnish

250 g (9 oz) fromage blanc
50 g (2 oz) shallots, peeled and chopped
15 g (½ oz) garlic, peeled and chopped
handful chives, finely snipped
handful parsley, chopped
250 ml (9 fl oz) double cream, whipped to soft peaks

FOR THE BLINIS
50 g (2 oz) buckwheat flour
½ litre (17½ fl oz) milk
30 g (1¼ oz) fresh yeast
250 g (9 oz) wholemeal flour
4 egg yolks
pinch sugar
4 egg whites
pinch salt
80 g (3¼ oz) unsalted butter

TO GARNISH
125 g (4½ oz) Oscietta caviar
fresh chervil

1. Place the fromage blanc in a piece of muslin, tie it securely with string, and suspend over a bowl for 24 hours.
2. Fold the shallot, garlic and herbs into the fromage blanc. Then fold in the whipped double cream. Refrigerate until required.
3. Place the buckwheat flour, milk and yeast in a pan and leave covered, at room temperature, for 1 hour. Add the wholemeal flour, egg yolks and a pinch of sugar, and leave covered for 2 hours.
4. Whisk the egg whites with a little salt until they peak. Fold them into the flour mixture and mix gently.
5. Cook the blinis one by one, on both sides, in a non-stick pan using a little of the butter at a time, until they are nicely coloured – 4 or 5 minutes in all. Put them on a wire rack and keep them warm.
6. To assemble and serve, put a blini on each plate. Using two dessert spoons, shape the fromage blanc into quenelles and place on top. Garnish with caviar and a chervil sprig.

blinis with caviar and fromage blanc

blinis and smoked salmon

blinis and smoked salmon

SERVES 4

See page 44.

tomato and anchovy tart

SERVES 4

I prefer to use fresh anchovies, but because they are small, delicate fish, and can quickly spoil, they are not that easily found outside Mediterranean fishing ports. For this recipe you can certainly use tinned anchovies instead. The inspiration for this recipe, of course, is the pizza, though the use of puff pastry makes it lighter and less yeasty. You can replace the anchovies with mozzarella cheese, or indeed any number of traditional pizza fillings.

300 g (10 oz) puff pastry (Basic 28)

flour for rolling

1 beaten egg to glaze

4 plum tomatoes, peeled

12 anchovy fillets, fresh or tinned

80 g (3¼ oz) block of Parmesan
   cheese

150 g (5 oz) rocket

4 tablespoons balsamic vinegar

4 tablespoons olive oil

salt and freshly ground black pepper

1. Preheat the oven to 200°C/400°F/Gas 6. Roll out the puff pastry on a lightly floured work surface, and cut it into four 11 x 11 cm (4½ x 4½ in) squares. With each of them, fold two opposite sides towards the centre, so you are left with four rectangles measuring 11 x 8 cm (4½ x 3¼ in). Prick the middles with a fork, place them on a baking sheet, and chill for 10 minutes.

2. Brush the pastry with the egg wash, and bake in the oven for 10 to 12 minutes until crisp and golden brown.

3. Quarter the peeled plum tomatoes and remove the seeds. Using a vegetable peeler, peel lengthways down the block of Parmesan to get shavings of cheese (you will need 5 to 8 strips per portion, about 30 in all).

4. Arrange the tomatoes and anchovies alternately on each puff pastry base. Put them back in the oven to warm the topping through.

5. Preheat the grill, lay half the Parmesan strips on the tarts, and grill for a few seconds.

6. Sort the rocket leaves, and trim any that are too long. Rinse them well in cold water and drain. Place them in a mixing bowl with the balsamic vinegar and olive oil, and season with salt and pepper. Divide the salad in four and place in a circle on each plate. Place a tart in the centre, and serve with a sprinkling of Parmesan shavings on top.

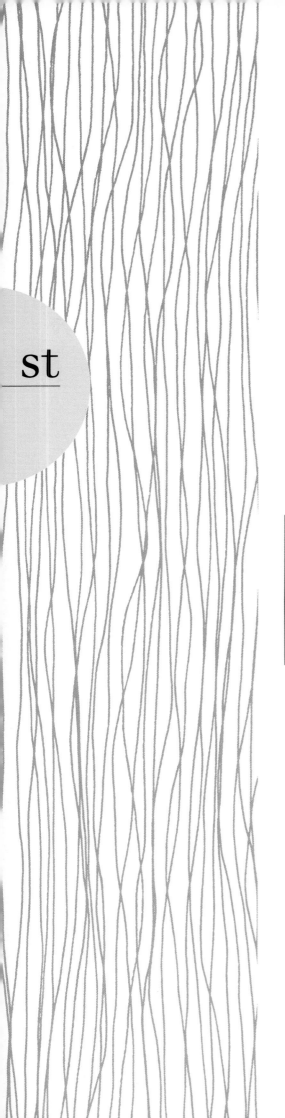

Salad of tomatoes and prawns

SERVES 4

Here is my version of that much-maligned old favourite, the prawn cocktail. The common pink prawn will do for this dish, but make sure if you buy them frozen that they are thoroughly defrosted, and if you buy them uncooked that you steam them thoroughly.

4 large beefsteak tomatoes
4 hard-boiled eggs
300 g (10 oz) shelled prawns
100 ml (3½ fl oz) Mary Rose sauce (Basic 13)
salt and freshly ground white pepper
a handful of chervil, chopped
a handful of chives, chopped
a handful of tarragon, chopped
60 ml (2¼ fl oz) fresh tomato sauce (Basic 14)
a handful of snipped chives
4 sprigs fresh chervil
cracked peppercorns and rock salt

1. Skin the tomatoes (the technique is to place them for about 30 seconds in water that has just boiled, and then refresh in cold water). Remove the stem in the eye side, and make a circle large enough to allow you to scoop out the seeds. Turn upside down and leave to dry.

2. Mix the eggs, cooked prawns and Mary Rose sauce, season to taste, and add the herbs. Put the mixture into the tomato shells. Put the lid back on, and spread a little tomato sauce around the base.

3. Arrange a few snipped chives around the edge of the sauce. Garnish the lid of each tomato with a sprig of fresh chervil, and season with cracked pepper and rock salt.

salad of tomatoes and prawns

tart of endive with sea scallops

SERVES 4

Rather confusingly, what we call chicory is what the French call *endive*; and what we call endive (see the recipe for Salad Lyonnaise, page 34) the French call *chicorée*. For this dish what we use at the Mirabelle is fresh chicory imported from Belgium. As for the scallops, you can get them fresh or frozen, though the latter may have lost some flavour.

200 g (8 oz) puff pastry (Basic 28)

4 heads chicory

1 orange

1 lemon

50 ml (2 fl oz) olive oil

12 coriander seeds

salt & pepper

30 g (1¼ oz) unsalted butter

pinch sugar

8 large sea scallops

chervil sprigs, to garnish

FOR THE DRESSING

100 ml (3½ fl oz) olive oil

1 shallot, finely chopped

1 large red pepper, peeled, de-seeded and finely chopped

100 ml (3½ fl oz) balsamic vinegar

10 g (¼ oz) chopped chives

salt & pepper

1. On a lightly floured surface, roll out the puff pastry to a 4 mm (¼ in) base, then chill in the fridge for about an hour.

2. Preheat the oven to 180°C/350°F/Gas 4. Cut the chicory in half. Squeeze the juice from the orange and lemon, and pour it over the chicory with a little of the olive oil. Crush the coriander seeds, and sprinkle them on top. Season, cover with tinfoil, and cook in the oven for 20 minutes until the chicory is tender.

3. In four non-stick dishes measuring about 10 cm (4 in) in diameter and 1 cm (½ in) deep, divide the butter evenly with a pinch of sugar. Drain the chicory, and arrange two halves, cut side down, in each dish. Heat until the chicory caramelises, then set aside and leave to cool.

4. Cut 4 rings from the pastry large enough to cover the dishes, and place these rings over the chicory. Leave to rest for about 1 hour. Then cook in the oven for 20 minutes until the pastry is pale golden.

5. Meanwhile, make the dressing. Heat the olive oil in a pan and sweat the shallot until soft. Add the red pepper, and cook gently for 1 more minute. Then add the balsamic vinegar and chives. Season, and keep warm.

6. Cut the scallops in half, and season them. Heat the remaining oil in a non-stick pan, and sauté the scallops for 30 seconds on each side.

7. Turn the tarts on to warm plates, and arrange the scallops neatly on top. Spoon the dressing around them, and garnish with chervil.

tarte tatin of caramelised onion and goat's cheese

tarte tatin of caramelised onion and goat's cheese

SERVES 4

If you have your puff pastry already made, this is a quick dish to produce and a popular starter. Any sort of goat's milk cheeses, which the French call *chèvres*, will do – and there is a huge variety, in all shapes and sizes, to choose from.

2 *large Spanish onions, skinned*
40 g (1½ oz) *unsalted butter*
40 g (1½ oz) *caster sugar*
200 g (8 oz) *puff pastry* (Basic 28)
100 g (4 oz) *goat's cheese*
rock salt
flat-leaf parsley to garnish

1. Preheat the oven to 200°C/400°F/Gas 6. Top and tail the onions, and cut them in half. For each onion half put 10 g (¼ oz) each of butter and sugar in a non-stick blini pan, and push the half onion into the butter. Place on a low heat, and slowly cook the onion until soft and golden brown. Remove from the stove, and allow to cool.

2. Roll out the puff pastry to make 4 discs 3 mm (⅛ in) thick and 130 mm (5 in) in diameter, and chill them.

3. In 10 cm (4 in) ramekins, place the puff pastry discs on top of the onion halves, and fold down the sides. Put each dish in the oven and cook for 15 to 20 minutes, until the pastry is golden brown.

4. Turn the tarts out on to plates, pouring over them any juices from the pans.

5. Place three thin slices of goat's cheese on top of each, and place briefly under a hot grill until the cheese starts to melt. Serve immediately, garnished with a little rock salt and parsley.

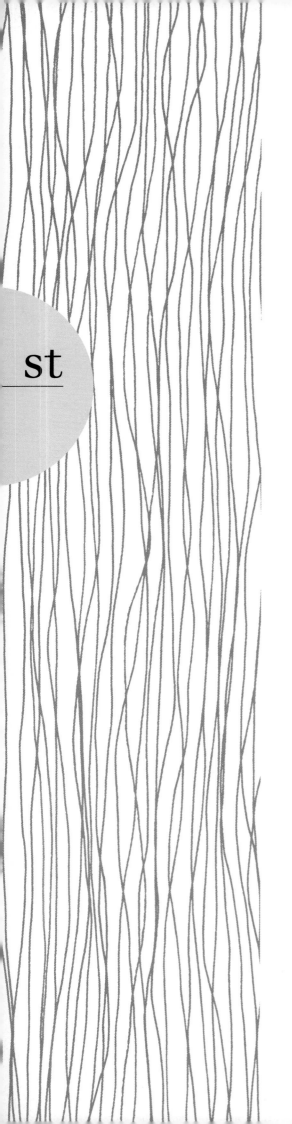

bayonne ham with celeriac remoulade

SERVES 4

Jambon de Bayonne comes from the Basses-Pyrénées in the far south-west of France, and is dry-cured and smoked. Get it sliced extremely thin. Celeriac is a delicious vegetable, tasting like a particularly sweet and nutty celery, and is available mainly in winter. This wonderful cold starter can be prepared in advance.

1 head celeriac
juice of 1 lemon
freshly ground salt
100 g (4 oz) mayonnaise (Basic 15)
1 teaspoon grain mustard
300 g (10 oz) thinly sliced Bayonne ham
freshly ground white pepper
20 drops truffle oil
4 sprigs chervil

1. Cut the celeriac into roughly even slices about 3 mm (¼ in) thick, peel each slice fairly thickly to get a smooth edge, and cut the slices into strips. Mix them with the lemon juice and a little salt, and leave them for 30 minutes to allow the water to come out of the celeriac.
2. Add the mayonnaise and mustard, and mix together.
3. Divide the ham into four and arrange it neatly on each plate, leaving the centre free.
4. Put the celeriac remoulade in the space in the centre of each plate, season with the pepper and truffle oil, and garnish with the chervil sprigs.

bayonne ham with celeriac remoulade

f

FISH DISHES

f

smoked haddock with poached egg and beurre blanc

Smoked haddock with poached egg and beurre blanc

SERVES 4

Haddock is cold-smoked, and its flesh should be moist and translucent, with a pale yellow surface and silvery-grey skin. Poaching is one of the best ways to cook it, but it must be done gently so that it doesn't fall apart in cooking. This dish has always been one of the most popular main courses at all my restaurants.

4 portions beurre blanc (Basic 9)
4 poached eggs
4 x 180 g (7 oz) pieces of naturally-smoked haddock with skin on
warm milk to cover
4 sprigs fresh chervil
4 portions bubble and squeak (Basic 26)

1. Make the beurre blanc and keep warm.
2. Bring a small pan of water to the boil, add a teaspoon of white wine vinegar, poach the eggs, and keep warm (for more detailed instructions, see the recipe for Poached Eggs Benedict, page 38).
3. Place the fish in a shallow pan and cover with warm milk. Cook for about 5 minutes, or until the fish starts to flake open and the skin peels off easily. Remove from the milk and peel off the skin.
4. Reheat the poached eggs by plunging them in boiling water for about 1 minute.
5. To serve, set the eggs on top of the haddock pieces, and spoon the beurre blanc over them. Garnish with chervil. Serve with new potatoes, bubble and squeak, or a salad if you prefer.

f

If serving with bubble and squeak, place a portion of bubble and squeak on each plate, followed by a piece of haddock, and set the egg on top. Spoon over the beurre blanc, and garnish with chervil.

fish and chips

SERVES 4

This favourite British dish depends on several things to be really good – the quality and freshness of the fish (I personally prefer haddock, though cod is as popular); the chips (which should be twice fried); and the kind of batter used (I like a mixture of beer and water, which makes a delicious light batter). The beer you use is up to you. We use Budvar lager. A stout will produce a stronger batter, but you will need to reduce the amount of fresh yeast you use with it.

4 x 200 g (8 oz) fillets haddock, pinboned and scaled, with skin on
a little seasoned flour
4 portions pea purée (Basic 27)
Lemon halves for garnish

FOR THE BATTER
1 x 330 ml (½ pint) bottle of beer
330 ml (11½ fl oz) cold water
20 g (¾ oz) fresh yeast
300 g (10 oz) plain flour

FOR THE CHIPS
8 large potatoes, peeled and cut into chips 4 cm x 1 cm x 1 cm (1½ x
* ½ x ½ in)*
oil for frying

1. Make the batter by mixing the beer, water and yeast together in a large bowl, and whisk well. Slowly add the flour, and whisk until smooth. Leave in a warm place for 20 minutes, to allow the yeast to ferment. Bubbles will cover the surface when it does. Whisk well before using.
2. Now heat the oil in a deep fat fryer to 150°C/300°F, and cook the chips until soft. Drain them on a clean cloth, and set aside.
3. Pass the fish through the seasoned flour, then dip in the batter. Cook them in a second deep fat fryer at 180°C/350°F for about 7 minutes until done.
4. Put the chips back in their fryer at the original temperature (150°C/300°F) and cook until they are crisp and golden brown. Serve with pea purée, garnished with lemon halves.

fish and chips

grilled lemon sole with tartare sauce

grilled lemon sole with tartare sauce

SERVES 4

The lemon sole suffers from the fact that it has 'sole' in its name. It is quite a different fish, plentiful, inexpensive, and with a delicate flavoursome white flesh with a wonderful texture. This simple dish couldn't be easier to do at home, and has been a great favourite at the Mirabelle – though more recently we have been doing the same recipe with Dover sole, for which, alas, we have to charge more but which takes less time to cook.

4 x 450 g (1 lb) lemon sole, trimmed and skinned
100 g (4 oz) seasoned flour
100 g (4 oz) unsalted butter

FOR THE TARTARE SAUCE
15 g (½ oz) mayonnaise (Basic 15)
20 g (¾ oz) shallots, finely diced and blanched
10 g (¼ oz) chopped capers
10 g (¼ oz) chopped gherkins
10 g (¼ oz) chopped parsley
juice of 1 lemon

1. Make the tartare sauce by placing the mayonnaise, shallot, capers, parsley and lemon juice in a bowl and mixing gently together. Keep at room temperature while cooking the fish.
2. Dip the sole in the seasoned flour, and shake to remove any excess. Heat the butter in a non-stick frying pan. Place the fish in the pan and cook until golden on both sides.
3. Serve with chips or new potatoes, and the tartare sauce. Garnish with half a lemon, and deep-fried parsley.

f

Cod mirabelle

SERVES 2

This is a new recipe, based on my finding a way to inject parsley and garlic butter into the centre of a fillet of cod. It is then floured, egged and breadcrumbed, and deep fried. The result is crispy and delicious, particularly when the garlic butter oozes out.

2 cloves garlic

1 bunch flat-leaf parsley, chopped

zest of ½ lemon

80 g (3¼ oz) unsalted butter, softened

1 kg (2 lb 3½ oz) cod, scaled and filleted, giving 2 x 180 g (7 oz) fillets

1 lemon, halved

4 small bunches watercress

pommes frites (Basic 24)

FOR THE COATING

50 g (2 oz) plain flour

2 eggs, beaten

150 g (5 oz) breadcrumbs

sunflower oil for deep frying

1. Crush the garlic to a fine paste, then add the chopped parsley, lemon zest and soft butter, and mix well. Place in a piping bag.

2. With a sharp filleting knife, cut a small slit under the skin of the cod, then pipe the garlic butter into the fish, being careful not to over-fill.

3. Dip the cod fillets first in seasoned flour, then in the beaten eggs, and finally in the breadcrumbs.

4. Preheat the sunflower oil to 160°C/320°F, and deep fry the cod until crisp and golden. Serve with pommes frites, and garnish the plates with half a lemon and a bunch of watercress.

cod mirabelle

fritto misto

SERVES 4

200 g (8 oz) cod, scaled and filleted

200 g (8 oz) salmon, scaled and filleted

200 g (8 oz) fresh haddock, scaled and filleted

200 g (8 oz) plaice, skinned and filleted

100 g (4 oz) squid, cleaned

4 tiger prawns, de-shelled and de-veined

juice 1 lemon

1 litre (33 fl oz) olive oil

50 g (2 oz) seasoned flour

2 eggs, beaten

200 g (8 oz) fine fresh white breadcrumbs

salt and freshly ground black pepper

FOR THE SAUCE BOIS BOUDRAN

150 ml (5½ fl oz) groundnut oil

50 ml (2 fl oz) white wine vinegar

salt and freshly ground black pepper

85 g (3½ oz) tomato ketchup

a teaspoon Worcestershire sauce

6 drops Tabasco

100 g (4 oz) shallots, chopped

a few chives, chopped

a little chervil, chopped

20 g (¾ oz) tarragon, chopped

Pané is the French term for coating a piece of meat or fish with flour, eggs and breadcrumbs. In this recipe I take a selection of fish and other seafood, pané them and shallow fry them, before serving them with bois boudran, one of my favourite sauces.

1. Cut the cod, salmon, haddock and plaice into four pieces, and the squid into rings. Place with the tiger prawns on a plate and squeeze a little lemon juice over.
2. Heat the olive oil in a pan. Dip the fish in the seasoned flour, beaten egg and breadcrumbs (in that order), then drop in the hot oil and cook until golden brown. Remove from the oil, and place on kitchen paper to remove the excess oil.
3. To make the sauce, combine the oil and vinegar with a pinch of salt and pepper in a bowl. Stir in the ketchup, Worcestershire sauce, Tabasco, shallots and all the chopped herbs. Keep at room temperature until needed.
4. Season the fritto misto, and serve with the sauce bois boudran.

Cod à l'indien

SERVES 2

Cod is a wonderfully versatile fish, which used to be plentiful and therefore relatively cheap. Alas this is no longer the case, so care needs to be taken in selecting it. Inshore cod, for example from Scarborough, is more flavoursome than deep-sea cod from remote northern waters, which will have been cleaned, gutted and frozen at sea to preserve it during the long trip back to port and to the market.

I serve this recipe with home-made tomato sauce (Basic 14), which uses a lot of tomatoes and takes quite a time to make – but it is also delicious with bought ketchup.

1 teaspoon curry powder
10 ml (⅓ fl oz) groundnut oil
1 kg (2 lb 3½ oz) cod, scaled and filleted, giving 2 x 180 g (7 oz) fillets
300 ml (10½ fl oz) sunflower oil
beer batter (see recipe for Fish and Chips, page 60)
2 lemons, halved
4 sprigs coriander
pommes frites (Basic 24)

1. Mix the curry powder and the groundnut oil, infuse over a low heat for 2 minutes, allow to cool, and paint it generously on the cod skin. Leave to marinate for 1 hour.
2. Preheat the sunflower oil to 180°C/350°F. Flour the cod, and dip in the beer batter. Place in the hot oil, and cook for 6 to 7 minutes until golden brown. Remove and drain on kitchen paper.
3. Serve with pommes frites, and garnish with half a lemon and fresh coriander.

fillet of whiting colbert

SERVES 4

200 g (8 oz) unsalted butter
30 g (1¼ oz) finely chopped parsley
15 g (½ oz) chopped shallots
10 g (¼ oz) finely chopped garlic
2 tablespoons Pernod
a few pinches of salt
a pinch of freshly ground white pepper
4 x butterflied whiting fillets
80 g (3¼ oz) seasoned flour
3 eggs, beaten
200 g (8 oz) fresh breadcrumbs
vegetable oil for deep frying
12 sprigs flat-leaf parsley, deep fried
2 lemons, halved
new potatoes (Basic 21)

Whiting is a member of the cod family, with a delicate flesh and flavour. They need to be very fresh if they are to be filleted and butterflied (cut down the back). Ask your fishmonger to do this. Use very fine home-made bread-crumbs for the coating

1. First make the garlic and herb butter. Beat together the butter, parsley, shallots, garlic, Pernod and some of the salt and pepper. On clingfilm, roll out the parsley butter mixture into a log about 4 cm (1½ in) in diameter, wrap it and chill in the fridge for about 30 minutes until it is set firm enough to slice.
2. Make sure all the bones have been removed from the fish. Dust with flour, and pass through the beaten egg and breadcrumbs (in that order) so the fish is evenly coated.
3. Preheat the grill to hot, and heat the deep fat fryer to 170°C/325°F. Add the fish, and cook for 6 to 8 minutes until golden. Drain and season with salt and pepper, then place a slice of butter on each fish and put briefly under the grill until it starts to melt. The dish goes well with new potatoes and a side salad.

f

omelette arnold bennett

Omelette arnold bennett

SERVES 4

This classic dish gets its name from the now rather unfashionable novelist of the potteries, who ate regularly at the Savoy Hotel in London and liked his omelettes cooked this way. It is one of the most popular starters we serve at the Mirabelle. To make our omelettes really special, I spread a mixture of 80 per cent Mornay sauce, 10 per cent lightly whipped cream and 10 per cent Hollandaise on top of the omelette before it goes under the grill. This is complicated, so you could alternatively add an extra egg yolk to the sauce, or sprinkle a little extra cheese on top before grilling.

FOR THE MORNAY SAUCE
15 g (½ oz) unsalted butter
15 g (½ oz) plain flour
200 ml (7 fl oz) warm milk
30 g (1¼ oz) Gruyère cheese, grated
a little English mustard
dash Worcestershire sauce
salt and freshly ground black pepper

TO COMPLETE
400 g (14 oz) undyed boned smoked haddock fillet
8 medium eggs
about 50 g (2 oz) unsalted butter
chervil, to garnish

1. Begin by making the Mornay sauce. Melt the butter in a pan, add the flour and cook for about 1 minute, stirring. Gradually whisk in the milk, and bring the roux sauce to the boil. Simmer for another minute, then remove from the heat, add the remaining ingredients and stir until all the cheese has melted.
2. Place the haddock slices on kitchen parchment, steam or grill until half cooked, and set aside in a warm place.
3. Make the omelettes separately. For each, beat 2 eggs in a bowl. Preheat a non-stick Teflon pan and add a knob of butter. When it has melted but is not sizzling, add the beaten eggs. Cook over a medium heat until the omelette is set on the bottom but still wet in the middle.
4. Preheat the grill to hot. Slide the omelette on to a heat-proof plate (wet side up), slide a slice of par-cooked haddock on top, then spread 2 tablespoons Mornay sauce over it. Flash under the hot grill until the top is just starting to turn golden. Serve garnished with fresh chervil.

f

tuna with aubergines, basil, tomato

and olive oil

SERVES 4

Tuna is an oily fish, with dense, firm meat. There are a number of species caught in temperate and subtropical seas, and so the colour can range from pale pink to dark red. There are all sorts of ways of cooking it, and this is the simplest – but the delicious Mediterranean accompaniments will take you rather more time.

baby fennel, trimmed
4 portions Sauce Vierge (Basic 8)
8 basil leaves, cut into julienne
1 medium-size tomato, skinned, de-seeded and finely diced
40 stoned black olives, halved
4 x 150 g (5 oz) tuna steaks
4 tablespoons olive oil
salt and freshly ground black pepper
tapenade (Basic 18)
a handful each of chervil, tarragon and chives
4 portions of Aubergine caviar (Basic 17)

1. Cook the baby fennel for 3 minutes in boiling salted water. Drain well and keep warm.
2. Gently reheat the Sauce Vierge, and add to it the julienne of basil, then the tomato, and the olive halves.
3. Season the tuna, heat the olive oil in a large non-stick frying pan, and fry the fish for about 3 minutes on each side.
4. Place the fish on each plate. Spread tapenade over each piece, spoon the sauce around, and decorate with the herbs, fennel and aubergine caviar, shaping the latter into oval quenelles using a dessert spoon.

tuna with aubergines, basil,
tomato and olive oil

Salmon fishcakes with sorrel and watercress sauce

SERVES 4

When most people think of fishcakes they think of potatoes, but at the Mirabelle we make ours without. Our fishcakes are a variation on a Russian dish called *pojarski*. I like to top them with a poached egg and serve with a herb sauce. To make it even richer, we sometimes top the egg with Hollandaise sauce.

Salmon is a wonderful fish, but it can be spoiled by overcooking. Wild salmon is firmer and more muscular, with a superior flavour to farmed salmon.

600 g (1 lb 5 oz) fresh salmon, skinned and boned

2 medium shallots, chopped

100 g (4 oz) soft unsalted butter

1 egg

50 g (2 oz) gherkins, finely diced

50 g (2 oz) capers, finely diced

zest of 1 lemon

1 bunch sorrel, coriander and flat parsley, cut into julienne

pinch cayenne pepper

dash Tabasco sauce

dash Worcestershire sauce

FOR THE BREADCRUMB COATING

2 eggs, beaten

50 g (2 oz) plain flour

150 g (5 oz) fresh breadcrumbs

300 ml (10½ fl oz) vegetable oil, for frying

FOR THE SORREL AND WATERCRESS SAUCE

30 g (1¼ oz) sorrel leaves

30 g (1¼ oz) watercress leaves

30 g (1¼ oz) unsalted butter

40 g (1½ oz) shallots, finely chopped

200 ml (7 fl oz) vegetable stock (Basic 7)

200 ml (7 fl oz) double cream

salt and freshly ground white pepper

4 poached eggs (see the recipe for Poached Eggs Benedict, page 38)

chervil sprigs

boiled potatoes (Basic 21)

1. Preheat the oven to 120°C/250°F/Gas ½. Place the salmon in buttered cooking foil, and cook in the oven for about 20 minutes until pink. Remove, and allow to cool. Coarsely flake the fish.

2. Cook the chopped shallots in a little butter until soft. Then combine all the ingredients – fish, shallots, egg, gherkins, capers, lemon zest, herb juliennes, cayenne, Tabasco and Worcestershire sauce – in a bowl and mix thoroughly. Add the soft butter, and leave to cool. Spoon the mixture into round moulds, or large pastry-cutters all the same size, and place them in the fridge for 30 minutes to set.

3. Lightly flour each fishcake, then dip in the egg mix followed by the breadcrumbs. Deep fry in the vegetable oil at 160°C/320°F until golden brown.

4. To make the sauce, wash the sorrel and watercress leaves. Melt the butter in a small pan and add the shallots. Sweat until soft. Add the sorrel and watercress, and cook for 1 minute. Add the vegetable stock, reduce by two-thirds, pour in the double cream and bring to the boil.

5. Remove from the heat, and blend the sauce in a liquidiser before passing it through a sieve. Season to taste.

6. To assemble, spoon a little sauce on each plate, set a fishcake on top followed by a poached egg and then a little more sauce. Garnish with fresh chervil, and serve with boiled potatoes.

salmon fishcakes with sorrel and watercress sauce

f

2 heads chicory

1 whole lemon

2 tablespoons olive oil

salt and freshly ground black pepper

2 oranges (zest, 4 segments, and squeeze the remaining juice)

2 grapefruits (4 segments, and squeeze the remaining juice)

2 more lemons (4 segments, and squeeze the remaining juice)

4 bay leaves

20 coriander leaves

4 x 250g (8 oz) black bream fillets

This recipe can also work well with red mullet or sea bass. Depending on the weight of the fish, the cooking time (see step 4) may need to be reduced.

Sea bream with citrus fruits

SERVES 4

Sea bream are not easy to find, in any of their many varieties, so buy them when you see them – they are not expensive, and the flesh is sweet, firm and delicate. This recipe is for the black bream, which is called red porgy in the USA but is actually dark grey. You need a fairly large specimen, so it can be filleted and pinboned. The recipe can also work well with red mullet.

1. Preheat the oven to 180°C/350°F/Gas 4. Cut the chicory heads in half and squeeze the lemon over them. Add 2 teaspoons of olive oil, and season. Cover in tinfoil and cook in the oven for about 20 minutes until the chicory is tender. (Reheat for 30 seconds while you are cooking the fish.)

2. Place 2 teaspoons of olive oil with 1 tablespoon of each of the fruit juices and the orange zest in a pan and bring to simmering point. Add the bay leaves and coriander, and keep hot on one side.

3. Arrange 3 of each of the fruit segments on each plate (nine segments per plate). Keep one segment of each to one side.

4. Slowly heat the remaining olive oil in a non-stick frying pan, adding the fish, skin side down, before the oil gets too hot, and cook for a minute or two until the skin is crispy, then 30 seconds on the other side.

5. To serve, put chicory in the centre of each plate, the fish on top (skin side up) and the three remaining fruit segments plus a bay leaf. Then spoon over the citrus sauce, and decorate with coriander.

f

wing of skate

Wing of skate with capers and balsamic vinegar dressing

SERVES 4

Skate has a delicious, sweet flavour, and is usually sold skinned on one side with a pearly white skin on the other. I buy 450 g (1 lb) wings which, when trimmed, make a portion of the right size. The acidity of the capers and lemons in this recipe, contrasting with the sweetness of the balsamic vinegar, really brings out the flavour of the skate.

4 x 450 g (1 lb) wings of skate
a little flour
100 ml (3½ fl oz) olive oil
8 lemon segments
4 tablespoons capers
4 tablespoons balsamic vinegar
flat-leaf parsley, to garnish

1. Preheat the oven to 220°C/425°F/Gas 7. Trim the skate wings and coat in a little flour. Heat 4 tablespoons of the olive oil in an oven-proof pan on the stove. Place the fish in the pan skin side down, and cook over a moderate heat for 3 to 5 minutes until caramelised.

2. Turn the fish over in the pan and place in the oven for about 20 minutes until done. When the fish comes away from the bone, it is cooked.

3. To serve, warm the capers in a pan with about 1 tablespoon of olive oil. Set each skate wing on a plate, scatter with warm capers and a lemon segment, whizz together the vinegar and remaining oil, and drizzle over the fish. Garnish with flat-leaf parsley.

f

grilled lobster with garlic and herb butter

SERVES 4

This is a variation on a recipe I published in an earlier book. You can make the stock and garlic and herb butter well in advance. The best fresh lobsters are from Scotland. You can buy them cooked, but they are much better live. We serve this dish with a side salad.

200 g (8 oz) unsalted butter

30 g (1¼ oz) finely chopped parsley

15 g (½ oz) chopped shallots

10 g (¼ oz) finely chopped garlic

2 tablespoons Pernod

a few pinches salt

a pinch freshly ground white pepper

4 x 600 g (1 lb 5 oz) native lobsters

1 carrot, chopped

1 stick celery, chopped

1 onion, chopped

1 bay leaf

1 sprig thyme

small handful parsley stalks

20 white peppercorns, crushed

½ litre (17½ fl oz) white wine

½ litre (17½ fl oz) white wine vinegar

10 litres (2½ gallons) water

salt

some sprigs of chervil or fresh parsley

The secret of this recipe is to work quickly, keeping the lobster at a constant temperature of 80°C/176°F right up to the last moment, when it goes into the hot oven.

1. First make the garlic and herb butter. Beat together the butter, parsley, shallots, garlic, Pernod and some of the salt and pepper. On clingfilm, roll out the parsley butter mixture into a log about 4 cm (1½ in) in diameter, wrap it and chill in the fridge for about 30 minutes until it is set firm enough to slice.

2. Make the stock. Put the carrot, celery, onion, bay leaf, thyme, parsley stalks, peppercorns, wine, vinegar and water into a large pot and simmer until all the vegetables are cooked. Turn off the heat and leave to stand for an hour. Sieve, and season with salt to taste.

3. Heat the stock to 80°C/176°F, take the bands off the lobster claws, and plunge the lobsters into the pan for 3½ minutes. Then remove them, wrap them in clingfilm, and set them aside in a warm place for 4 or 5 minutes to relax.

4. Remove the claws from the bodies, and crack them open and take out the meat. Also remove the meat from the knuckles and set aside. With a large, sharp chopping knife, cut the lobsters in half lengthways, and remove the meat, discarding the brain sac. Clean out the lobster shells.

5. Place the garlic butter in a piping bag, and pipe a small amount of the butter inside the shell from end to end. Cut the body meat into 3 or 4 pieces, and place them back in the opposite side of the shell, so that the red of the meat shows. Put the knuckle and claw meat into the brain cavities, and lightly cover with garlic butter.

6. Heat a roasting dish, put the lobsters on it and place in a hot oven (200°C/400°F/Gas 6) for 2 to 3 minutes. Don't let the butter burn.

7. Arrange on a plate and decorate with the chervil or parsley. We also add a little Béarnaise sauce (Basic 11) on the lobster meat.

grilled lobster with garlic and herb butter

m

Meat & Game

m

roast chicken

roast chicken

SERVES 4

Here is what we serve as roast chicken à l'Anglais, our version of the traditional English way of roasting a chicken. Normally at home one chicken (larger than the ones used in this recipe) will serve four, but we take the breasts and thighs off the bone before serving these quite generous portions.

2 x 1.3 kg (3 lb) free-range chickens
salt and freshly ground white pepper
100 ml (3½ fl oz) vegetable oil
4 portions haricots verts
4 portions pomme fondant (Basic 23)
500 ml (17½ fl oz) jus rôti (Basic 4)

1. Preheat the oven to 200°C/400°F/Gas 6. Heat the oil in a pan, season the chickens, and seal them all over in the hot oil.

2. Roast the chickens in the oven for about 35 minutes, then take them out and allow to rest for 10 minutes.

3. Carefully remove the breasts and legs. Trim the legs by cutting the knuckle and separating the thigh from the leg, discarding the foot.

4. Blanch the haricots verts in boiling salted water for about 4 minutes. Toss in an emulsion of butter and water.

5. Heat through the potatoes and the jus rôti.

6. To serve, place a chicken breast and thigh at the bottom of the plate and the haricots verts and pomme fondant at the top. Pour the hot jus rôti around.

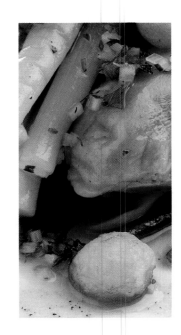

Chicken à la vinaigrette

SERVES 2

It is much easier than it used to be to find a chicken that actually tastes of something, that hasn't been intensively raised. They cost a bit more, of course, but the difference is really worth it. The best chicken, to my mind, are poulets de Bresse, from Burgundy in France, but free-range chickens generally and corn- or maize-fed birds always taste better than broilers.

1 x 1.5 kg (3 lb 4½ oz) free-range chicken
15 g (½ oz) unsalted butter, softened
200 g (8 oz) green beans
100 ml (3½ fl oz) vinaigrette (Basic 20)
2 medium potatoes
1 shallot, chopped
1 tablespoonful chopped parsley
50 g (2 oz) pan-roasted hazelnuts (optional)

1. Preheat the oven to 200°C/400°F/Gas 6. Prepare the chicken by taking out the wishbone and removing the legs and winglets (the latter can be used for making stock).
2. Moisten the breast and thighs with the softened butter and fry in a pan for about 15 minutes until golden.
3. Cover the chicken in foil, and roast in the preheated oven for 15 to 20 minutes until cooked through. Leave to rest for 8 to 10 minutes.
4. Cook the beans in boiling water until tender, then drain well. Cook the unpeeled potatoes until tender, then skin and slice into rounds.
5. Take the chicken off the bone, and slice it widthways into 3 or 4 pieces. Lightly toss the chicken, followed by the beans, potatoes, shallot, parsley and hazelnuts (if using) in the vinaigrette.
6. Arrange the beans in the centre of each plate and set the chicken on top – with a thigh underneath each breast. Arrange the potato slices around, scatter with hazelnuts, shallot and parsley, and pour any remaining vinaigrette over.

m

chicken à la vinaigrette

m

bang bang chicken

SERVES 4

This dish is a great favourite with customers at my most recent venture, the Titanic restaurant in London's West End. It consists basically of poached chicken breasts coated in a spicy peanut sauce and served sprinkled with sesame seeds on a bed of sliced cucumber. The inspiration, obviously, is far eastern.

2 skinless chicken breasts
200 ml (7 fl oz) chicken stock (Basic 1)
1 stick lemon grass, sliced
2 cloves garlic, crushed
1 small handful coriander stalks
1 knob root ginger, peeled and sliced
200 ml (7 fl oz) soy sauce
100 g (4 oz) smooth peanut butter
Tabasco to taste
3 spring onions
1 cucumber, peeled and seeded
toasted sesame seeds, to garnish

1. Poach the chicken breasts in the stock, lemon grass, garlic, coriander stalks, root ginger and soy sauce for 8 to 10 minutes. Remove the pan from the heat and leave the chicken in the liquor to cool.

2. Drain the chicken, straining and reserving the liquor, and slice the breasts very thinly.

3. Whisk the peanut butter with enough strained liquor to make a pouring consistency. Add Tabasco to taste.

4. Finely slice the spring onions lengthways, and cut the cucumber into julienne (matchstick strips). Lightly dress them with a little extra soy sauce, and arrange them on each plate.

5. Put chicken slices on top of the onion and cucumber juliennes, and pour the peanut sauce over them. Garnish with toasted sesame seeds.

To make your game chips more professional-looking, you can use the serrated blade of a mandolin. Adjust the blade so it is not quite shredding the potato, and keep turning the potato through 90° so you get slices with a grid. It's tricky, so watch your fingers!

roast pheasant properly garnished

SERVES 4

Of course the best pheasant is one you have shot, hung, plucked, drawn and trussed yourself. Otherwise, look for a brace of plump birds with a full skin that is not ripped. Freshly shot birds, at their best in November and December, should hang for at least three days for a good flavour to develop, and for as long as three weeks if the weather is very cold.

8 slices streaky bacon
2 x 1.1 kg (2½ lb) dressed pheasants
6 sprigs thyme
12 juniper berries
salt and freshly ground white pepper
goose fat for roasting
4 slices back bacon

FOR THE GRAVY
1 celery stick, chopped
1 onion, peeled and chopped
1 carrot, peeled and chopped
2 cloves garlic, peeled and halved
100 ml (3½ fl oz) white wine
thyme sprigs
200 ml (7 fl oz) veal stock (Basic 2)
salt and pepper

bread sauce (Basic 16)
4 portions chips (Basic 25)

1. Preheat the oven to 200°C/400°F/Gas 6. Arrange the slices of streaky bacon across each pheasant, and into each bird put the thyme and juniper berries, and season them inside and out. Then tie and truss them.
2. Heat the goose fat in a roasting tin on top of the stove, then seal the pheasants on all sides. Place the tin in the oven and roast the birds for 25 to 30 minutes (depending on their size). Remove and allow them to rest in a warm place.
3. Grill or pan-fry the back bacon, and keep warm.
4. Make the gravy, as follows. Place the cut celery, onion, carrot and garlic in the tin in which the pheasants were cooked, and roast them to a nice golden colour. Add the wine, thyme and a little salt and pepper, and boil until the liquid has virtually evaporated. Add the veal stock, and any juices that have come off the pheasants. Bring this to the boil and simmer for 3 minutes. Pass through a sieve into a gravy boat.
5. To serve, remove the pheasants' legs, trim the feet, and make a cut between the thigh and the drum stick. Then remove the breasts, and slice each into three. Place the slices of breast on top of a thigh and a drumstick. Serve the bread sauce, gravy, bacon and game chips separately, so people can help themselves. Popular accompaniments are Brussels sprouts, braised cabbage or roast parsnips.

m

Calf's liver and bacon

Calf's liver is fine and delicate in flavour, and much used in Italian cooking (particularly *Fegato alla veneziana*). Here is a more traditionally English way of serving it.

SERVES 4

vegetable oil
12 sage leaves
salt and freshly ground white pepper
4 small lettuces, Cos or Baby Gem
carrot, celeriac, onion and celery stalk, peeled and finely diced
25 g (1 oz) unsalted butter
250 ml (12 fl oz) veal stock (Basic 2)
8 very thin slices streaky bacon
plain flour
4 x 150 g (5 oz) thin slices calf's liver
4 portions pomme purée (Basic 22)

1. Deep-fry the sage leaves in hot vegetable oil, then drain well on kitchen paper. Season with a little salt.
2. Make the braised lettuce: halve the lettuces and blanch them quickly in boiling salted water, then refresh in cold water and drain well. Sweat the vegetable dice in the butter until they colour. Place the lettuce and diced vegetables in a pot and add the stock and some seasoning. Bring to the boil, cover, and braise for 10 to 15 minutes until tender.
3. Lightly grill the bacon without colouring.
4. Season and flour the liver, dusting off any excess. Pan-fry in 100 ml (3½ fl oz) hot oil until pink, a minute or so on each side depending on the thickness.
5. To serve, place the liver on a heap of braised lettuce, with two slices of bacon on top, and decorate with the sage. Serve with pomme purée.

m

calf's liver and bacon

Veal holstein

SERVES 4

This classic German way of presenting veal escalopes needs careful handling. It is important not to over-fry the egg, because the wetness of the yolk acts as a sauce for the rest of the dish.

4 x 150 g (5 oz) veal steaks
8 eggs
100 g (4 oz) seasoned flour
200 g (8 oz) fine breadcrumbs
2 tomatoes
200 g (8 oz) clarified butter
100 g (4 oz) unsalted butter
8 tablespoons veal jus (Basic 3)
40 small capers
4 small bundles watercress

At the Mirabelle we garnish the eggs with anchovies, to add a little extra zip.

1. Trim any fat from the steaks, place them in a clear plastic bag, and beat them with a meat bat until they are about 3½ mm (¼ in) thick.
2. Break and mix 4 of the eggs and place on a plate. Place the flour and breadcrumbs on two other plates. Dip the veal lightly in the flour, and then into the eggs and breadcrumbs.
3. Halve the tomatoes, grill them, and keep warm.
4. Heat half the clarified butter in a frying pan, add the veal steaks and cook them for 1½ to 2 minutes until golden. Turn them over and cook for another 1½ minutes. Remove from the pan, and keep them warm.
5. Fry the eggs gently in the remaining clarified butter, without over-cooking them.
6. Put the hard butter into a hot pan so it slowly starts to foam and darken, and heat the veal jus in another pan.
7. To serve, put the veal steaks on plates, with an egg on top. Pour a little jus and brown butter around them. Garnish with capers, watercress and grilled tomatoes.

m

Corned beef hash with fried eggs and HP sauce

SERVES 4

Here is another favourite from the Titanic (see Bang Bang Chicken), which we serve as part of our special breakfast menu from 11.30 pm to 2.30 am each night. Many of our guests enjoy drinking a Bloody Mary with this, although some prefer champagne. Either way, HP sauce is a great accompaniment.

1 medium onion, finely sliced
250 g (9 oz) clarified butter
600 g (1 lb 5 oz) corned beef
freshly ground salt and pepper
2 large potatoes, peeled
8 eggs
1 bunch watercress
HP sauce

1. Sweat the onion in 30 g (1¼ oz) of clarified butter and cook until softened but not coloured.
2. Take a fork and break up the corned beef. Season it lightly with salt and pepper, add the onion, and divide the mixture into 8 portions. Shape each into a ball.
3. Using a mandolin, slice the potatoes into straws. Lightly salt them and leave for 5 minutes in a colander or sieve. Then put them in a cloth and squeeze out the remaining water. Mix the potatoes with half the remaining clarified butter.
4. Preheat the oven to 190°C/375°F/Gas 5. Take each ball of corned beef and completely encase in potato, but not too thickly, moulding it in your hand. Once all 8 are ready, heat a non-stick pan and gently colour them, pressing down gently to form a disc shape. No oil or butter is needed in the pan, because fat comes out of the beef and potatoes. When nicely coloured, place them in the oven for 8 to 10 minutes to heat thoroughly.
5. While the hash is in the oven, heat the rest of the clarified butter gently in a non-stick pan and fry the eggs. Finish them with a little salt and pepper.
6. To serve, place an egg on top of each hash brown, garnish with a sprig of watercress, and serve with a dollop of HP sauce.

corned beef hash with
fried eggs and HP sauce

steak au poivre

Steak au poivre

SERVES 6

75 ml (3 fl oz) Worcestershire sauce
150 ml (5½ fl oz) double cream
6 x 200 g (8 oz) rump steaks
a pinch of salt
100 g (4 oz) whole black peppercorns,
*   crushed*
75 g (3 oz) clarified unsalted butter
watercress to garnish
pommes frites (Basic 24)

1. Put the Worcestershire sauce in a pan and boil for several minutes until reduced. Take off the heat, add the cream, and simmer until the sauce has thickened.

2. Sprinkle each side of the steaks with salt, and rub in. Then place the ground peppercorns on a plate, and press one side of each steak into them.

3. Heat the clarified butter in a large non-stick frying pan until sizzling. Add the steaks and pan fry for 2 to 3 minutes on each side. Spoon the sauce over the steaks, and serve with watercress garnish and pommes frites.

m

grilled rib-eye steak with snails and garlic butter

SERVES 4

The rib eye is an American cut of beef, taken from the eye of the rib, with the bone, fat and coarser meat removed. For this recipe you can use tinned snails – you'll need five per person.

200 g (8 oz) unsalted butter
30 g (1¼ oz) finely chopped parsley
15 g (½ oz) finely chopped shallots
10 g (¼ oz) finely chopped garlic
2 tablespoons Pernod
a pinch of salt
freshly ground white pepper
4 x 200 g (8 oz) rib-eye steaks
20 pre-cooked snails

1. Beat together the butter, parsley, shallots, garlic, Pernod and a little salt and pepper. On clingfilm, roll out the parsley butter mixture into a log about 4 cm (1½ in) in diameter, wrap it and chill in the fridge for about 30 minutes until it is set firm enough to slice.
2. Season the steaks with salt and pepper, heat a non-stick pan to red hot, and cook the steaks for about 3 minutes on each side. When they are done, put a generous slice of the parsley butter on top of each and place under a hot grill until the butter has melted.
3. Quickly heat the snails in the remaining parsley butter.
4. When the snails are piping hot, arrange five of them on each steak. You can serve this with grilled tomatoes and watercress, mushrooms and pommes frites (Basic 24).

Snails are still difficult to find in British shops, even tinned. There are a few suppliers, and if you want fresh snails you will have to seek one out. Alternatively, look for tinned snails in brine – though they will tend to be more chewy than fresh ones.

grilled rib-eye steak with snails and garlic butter

steak and eggs with HP sauce

Steak and eggs with HP sauce

SERVES 4

For this dish I use rib-eye steaks (see the recipe for Grilled Rib-eye Steak, page 96). They are the best quality you can buy at a reasonable price, though you can push the boat out and use fillet or sirloin if you prefer.

4 x 200 g (8 oz) rib-eye steaks
salt and freshly ground black and white pepper
100 ml (3½ fl oz) vegetable oil
50 g (2 oz) clarified butter
4 eggs
4 tomatoes, halved and grilled
8 field mushrooms, grilled
bunch watercress
4 portions pomme fondant (Basic 23)
HP sauce

1. Season the steaks with salt and white pepper. Heat the oil in a non-stick pan until red hot, and cook the steaks for 2 to 3 minutes on each side until golden brown (medium rare).
2. Heat the clarified butter in another non-stick pan, and fry the eggs. Finish them with a little salt and black pepper.
3. Place an egg on top of each steak, and garnish with grilled tomatoes and watercress, mushrooms and pomme fondant. Serve with HP sauce.

Cottage pie with pea purée

SERVES 6

In my restaurants I like to serve this traditional dish in individual oven-proof dishes, accompanied by another great English favourite, pea purée. It's simple, and absolutely delicious. Of course it is just as good done the usual way in a single oven-proof casserole or dish.

1 kg (a bit more than 2½ lb) minced beef
5 tablespoons vegetable oil
2 onions, chopped
1 clove garlic
400 g (14 oz) tinned chopped tomatoes
1 tablespoon tomato purée
500 ml (17½ fl oz) white wine
500 ml (17½ fl oz) veal jus (Basic 3)
sprig thyme
½ bay leaf
salt and freshly ground black pepper
500 g (1 lb 1 oz) mashed potatoes (pomme purée, Basic 22)
100 g (4 oz) grated Cheddar cheese
6 portions pea purée (Basic 27)

1. Brown the mince in half the oil in a hot pan. Drain off the fat and set aside.
2. Sweat the onions in the remaining oil until softened but not coloured. Add the garlic, and cook for a further minute. Add the chopped tomatoes and tomato purée and cook for 5 more minutes.
3. Add the white wine, and cook until reduced by two-thirds.
4. Preheat the oven to 180°C/350°F/Gas 4. Add the veal jus, thyme and bay leaf to the pan, and bring to the boil. Mix in the browned mince, and season with salt and pepper. Simmer for 30 minutes.
5. When cooked, place the mixture in an oven-proof dish (or individual dishes), cover with the mashed potatoes, sprinkle with the cheese and cook in the preheated oven until golden brown. Serve with pea purée quenelles, shaped with two dessert spoons, each with a little fresh mint on top.

m

lamb à la ficelle

SERVES 4

This is a really great spring dish. It's best if you make the stock yourself, although it takes time and trouble – and you can freeze what you don't need for this recipe and use it for making gravies or as the base for a good sauce – or indeed, serve it as consommé. Otherwise, use bought beef consommé.

FOR THE STOCK

1 beef shin, sliced into 5

½ calf's foot or pig's trotter

½ large ox tongue

½ boiling chicken

½ scorched onion

1 carrot

1 leek

10 sliced button mushrooms

20 black peppercorns

500 ml (17½ fl oz) Madeira, simmered to reduce by one quarter

200 ml (7 fl oz) soy sauce

1 tablespoon tomato purée

10 g (¼ oz) rock salt

3 cloves

2 x 400 g (14 oz) rumps of lamb

1 bunch baby leeks

1 bunch baby carrots

900 g (2 lb) new potatoes

250 g (9 oz) fresh peas

25 g (1 oz) baby red chard, optional

100 g (4 oz) asparagus

1. To make the stock, place the beef shin in the bottom of a deep pan with the calf's foot, tongue and boiling chicken. Place all the vegetables, peeled but whole, on top, and add the reduced Madeira. Place all the other stock ingredients in the pan, followed by just enough cold water to cover. Bring to the boil and simmer for 6 to 7 hours. Strain the hot stock carefully through muslin. Skim off the fat, and reserve.

2. Bring 750 ml (26½ fl oz) of the stock to the boil (the rest can be cooled and frozen). Heat a dry non-stick pan. Put in the lamb, fat side down, and cook briskly for 5 minutes until brown on all sides. Transfer the lamb to the stock, and cook for 8 to 10 minutes. Remove the lamb from the stock, and set it aside in a warm place to rest.

3. Prepare the baby vegetables: trim the green from the leeks, peel and cut the stalks from the carrots. Cook all the vegetables in boiling salted water for 5 to 8 minutes, adding the asparagus for the last few minutes.

4. To serve, arrange the cooked vegetables in four bowls, slice the lamb, and arrange it on top of the vegetables.

m

lamb à la ficelle

m

spring lamb provençale

Spring lamb provençale

SERVES 4

A rack of lamb (otherwise known as best end of neck, or a *carré d'agneau* in French) usually serves 2 people. Ask your butcher to chine and clean the bones for you.

> 2 x 6-rib racks of lamb, trimmed
> salt and freshly ground black pepper
> 4 tablespoons vegetable oil
> 1 tablespoon clarified butter
> 1 shallot, finely chopped
> 1 clove garlic, finely chopped
> 50 g (2 oz) dried white breadcrumbs
> 10 g (¼ oz) chopped fresh parsley
> 1 tablespoon chopped fresh thyme
> 200 g (8 oz) green beans, topped and tailed
> 50 g (2 oz) unsalted butter
> 2 tablespoons Dijon mustard
> 4 portions pomme fondant (Basic 23)
> jus rôti (Basic 4)

1. Preheat the oven to 180°C/350°F/Gas 4. Season the lamb, put the oil in a pan and cook the lamb briefly in the hot oil on a medium heat to seal in the juices. Transfer to the oven and cook for 30 to 45 minutes, depending on how big the lamb is, whether it is new or old season, and according to taste. When done, leave it to rest for 10 minutes.

2. Heat the clarified butter and sweat the shallot and garlic. Take off the heat, and stir in the breadcrumbs, parsley and thyme. Season.

3. Bring a pan of salted water to the boil. Add the beans, and simmer for 5 minutes. Then melt the butter in another pan, add the beans with a little of their water, season, and cook gently for another 1 to 2 minutes.

4. Preheat the grill to hot. Brush the rind of the lamb generously with the mustard, then pack on the herb and breadcrumb mixture. Place the lamb racks under the grill and cook until the crumbs start to colour.

5. Slice the lamb chops and arrange them on plates with the green beans and pomme fondant. Drizzle with jus rôti.

m

p

Puddings

We vary this dish by adding additional fruits, like banana and grapefruit. Put the raspberry layer in first as before, then some jelly, then sliced bananas, then more jelly, then some grapefruit segments, topped up with jelly.

p

raspberries in pink champagne jelly

SERVES 6

The best thing about these jellies is that they can be made in advance. Make sure your raspberries are really fresh – they come on to the market in June or July, followed by another crop as late as October. Any you have left over can be made into a simple raspberry coulis to serve with the jelly; or this light and refreshing dessert can just as well be served with double cream. You will need a set of six suitable 150 ml (5½ fl oz) pudding moulds.

1 bottle pink champagne
600 g (1 lb 5 oz) caster sugar
9 leaves gelatine
6 punnets raspberries
sprigs and extra raspberries to decorate
raspberry coulis (Basic 31) or double cream

1. Place the pink champagne and sugar in a pan and bring to the boil. While this is heating up, put the gelatine in ice-cold water.
2. When the champagne mixture reaches boiling point, take off the heat and add the soaked gelatine. Stir slowly, and allow to cool a little.
3. Pour a 2 mm (¾ in) layer of jelly into each mould, put in the fridge and allow them to set.
4. Now place a layer of raspberries in the bottom of the moulds. Pour in a little more jelly and replace in the fridge to set. Keep doing this until the moulds are full. Chill them until thoroughly set.
5. To serve, turn them out on plates and decorate with a sprig of fresh mint. Add raspberry coulis or cream as you prefer.

raspberries in pink champagne jelly

Whisky jelly with red fruits

SERVES 6

½ bottle of whisky
250 ml (9 fl oz) water
400 g (14 oz) caster sugar
7 leaves gelatine
2 punnets raspberries
2 bananas
1 punnet blackberries
1 punnet blueberries

This makes a very pretty dessert for midsummer. You will need a set of six suitable 150 ml (5½ fl oz) pudding moulds. Don't worry about the bananas turning black – the alcohol in the whisky prevents this.

1. Place the whisky, water and sugar in a pan and bring to the boil.

2. While the whisky mixture is heating up, place the gelatine in ice-cold water. When the whisky mixture reaches boiling point, take it off the heat and add the soaked gelatine. Stir slowly. Allow to cool a little.

3. Pour into each mould about 2 cm (⅛ in) of jelly, and place them in the fridge to set. Keep the rest of the jelly warm.

4. When the moulds are set, place the raspberries to fill the width of the mould, upside down, and add a little jelly – but don't cover the raspberries. Place back in the fridge to set.

5. When set, cover the raspberries with jelly and allow to set again.

6. Slice the bananas really finely, and place evenly on top of the raspberries. Cover with jelly and allow to set again. Repeat this process with the blackberries and blueberries (if the blackberries are too large, slice them in half).

7. Chill the moulds thoroughly until they are set. Turn them out and serve.

Sherry trifle

SERVES 6

Here's an old English favourite! I make my trifles using a home-made sherry-flavoured jelly, and tinned fruit to soak a home-made sponge. But you can buy quite good basic sponge in many supermarkets. You'll need 6 large stemmed cocktail glasses that taper downwards slightly.

1 tin pear halves, diced into 5 mm (¼ in) squares

1 tin peach halves, diced into 5 mm (¼ in) squares

18 discs of 5 mm (¼ in) sponge, 6 of them 20 mm (¾ in) and 12 of
*   them 30 mm (1⅛ in) in diameter (Basic 29)*

a few chopped roasted nuts and fresh raspberries to decorate

FOR THE JELLY

½ bottle medium sweet sherry

150 ml (5½ fl oz) water

150 g (5 oz) caster sugar

4 leaves gelatine, soaked

FOR THE CUSTARD

12 egg yolks

200 g (8 oz) caster sugar

500 ml (17½ fl oz) milk

1 tablespoon Bird's Custard Powder

FOR THE CRÈME CHANTILLY

500 ml (17½ fl oz) milk

100 g (4 oz) caster sugar

few drops vanilla essence

1. Mix the sherry, water and sugar in a pan and bring to the boil. Add the gelatine, and then allow to cool.

2. Combine the egg yolks and sugar. Bring the milk and cream to boiling point, and pour over the egg yolk mixture. Return to the stove and cook over a very low heat (no more than 80°C/176°F), stirring continuously using a wooden spoon. Add the custard powder and whisk until slightly thickened. Allow to cool.

3. Place a small disc of sponge in the bottom of each of 6 cocktail glasses, with a spoonful of the fruit (pears and peaches) on top. Pour on some of the jelly, and place in the fridge to set. Repeat this process until the glasses are filled up to 2.5 cm (1 in) from the top.

4. Place a large sponge disc on the top of each. Spoon on a layer of custard.

5. Pipe the crème chantilly on top of each trifle, and add a few roasted nuts and fresh raspberries.

p

panacotta

p

Panacotta

SERVES 4

Panacotta is a classic Italian pudding mainly made of cream flavoured with vanilla. It's delicious, and looks very pretty decorated with fresh raspberries and raspberry coulis (Basic 31), and a sprig of mint, as in the photograph opposite.

2 leaves gelatine
500 ml (17½ fl oz) double cream
80 g (3¼ oz) caster sugar
3 vanilla pods, sliced along the middle
2 tablespoons rum

1. Place the gelatine leaves in cold water to soften.
2. Add the sugar to the cream in a saucepan, with the split vanilla pods, and heat to just below boiling point.
3. Remove from the stove, stir in the softened gelatine and the rum, and pass through a fine sieve into 4 150 ml (5½ fl oz) pudding moulds. Place in the fridge for at least 4 hours to set.

Before you pour the mixture into the moulds, put it all in a bowl into the fridge and stir every two or three minutes for 20 minutes. This will make sure the vanilla seeds float evenly through the panacotta, rather than sink to the bottom.

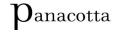

Always serve a soufflé the moment it comes out of the oven — and never open the oven door, however tempted you may be to see how it is getting on!

raspberry soufflé

SERVES 4

I have published this recipe before, but it is such a favourite at the Mirabelle that I cannot resist including it here.

50 g (2 oz) unsalted butter

16 fresh raspberries

125 ml (4½ fl oz) Framboise (raspberry eau de vie)

500 ml (17 fl oz) raspberry purée, sieved

15 g (½ oz) cornflour

320 g (11¾ oz) caster sugar

100 ml (3½ fl oz) water

12 egg whites

icing sugar

1. Preheat the oven to 180°C/350°F/Gas 4, and thoroughly grease 4 soufflé dishes measuring 7.5 cm (3 in) in diameter and 6.25 cm (2½ in) deep with half the butter.

2. Marinate the fresh raspberries in the Framboise until ready to use.

3. Make a raspberry reduction by placing the sieved purée in a pan and reducing it by half. Dissolve the cornflour in 25 ml (½ oz) of the Framboise, and add this to the reduced purée. Stir and cook until thickened, then remove from the heat. Mix 100 g (4 oz) of the sugar with the water, and boil up to 120°C/250°F. Add to the raspberry mixture, mix in well, and leave to cool.

4. Put the egg whites into the bowl of your mixer and begin to beat. When they start to take shape, begin adding the rest of the sugar, 50g (2 oz) at a time until each batch is thoroughly mixed in.

5. Put the cooled raspberry reduction in a round bowl, and whisk in a third of the beaten egg white, to loosen it. Fold in the remaining egg white carefully.

6. Half fill the soufflé dishes with the mixture, then place three drained marinated raspberries in the centre. Fill to the top with the mixture, then scrape off evenly with a palette knife. Run your finger round the edge to push the mixture away from the sides. Cook in the preheated oven for 10 minutes.

7. To serve, place the dish on a plate, dust with a little icing sugar, and put a raspberry on top. Serve with raspberry coulis (Basic 31) on the side.

raspberry soufflé

p

biscuit glacé aux noisettes

biscuit glacé aux noisettes

SERVES 12

425 g (15 oz) caster sugar
15 g (½ oz) shelled hazelnuts
6 egg whites
450 ml (16 fl oz) double cream
8 portions raspberry coulis (Basic 31)
60 fresh raspberries
12 sprigs mint

1. Line a terrine measuring 30 x 7.5 cm (12 x 3 in) with greaseproof paper, and put in the freezer at its coldest setting.
2. Make the praline as follows. Heat 150 g (5 oz) of the sugar in a pan until it melts and begins to make a caramel. Stir in the hazelnuts. Pour the mixture on to a cold, oiled tray to set, and when it is hard crush it into pieces.
3. Whip the egg whites and gradually add the remaining sugar to make a stiff meringue. Separately whip the cream until it makes stiff peaks. Then fold the whipped cream into the meringue and mix in the crushed praline.
4. Fill the ice-cold terrine to the top with the biscuit mixture, and place it back in the freezer until hard.
5. Meanwhile, make the raspberry coulis (Basic 31).
6. To serve, remove the terrine from the freezer and the biscuit from the terrine. Cut into 2.5 cm (1 in) slices. Put a slice on each plate, surround with raspberry coulis, and decorate each portion with 5 raspberries and a sprig of mint.

p

Vanilla crème brûlée

SERVES 10

175 g (6½ oz) caster sugar

9 egg yolks

4 vanilla pods

100 ml (3½ fl oz) milk

900 ml (31½ fl oz) double
   cream

demerara sugar

8 portions raspberry coulis
   (Basic 31)

20 fresh raspberries

In the photograph (opposite) we have decorated the crème brûlée with apple crisps – but it goes with any seasonal fruits.

1. Mix the sugar and egg yolks together in a bowl.
2. Split the vanilla pods in half and scrape the seeds out. Add the seeds to the milk and cream in a pan, plus the pods too. Heat gently so that the full flavour of the vanilla infuses the liquid.
3. Pour the cream and milk on to the sugar and yolk mixture, mix well, and pass through a conical strainer. Preheat the oven to 140°C/275°F/Gas 1.
4. Fill 10 ramekins (roughly 7.5 cm (3 in) in diameter) with the mixture, and cook them in a bain-marie of hot water in the preheated oven for 30 to 40 minutes until just set.
5. Allow the ramekins to cool, then chill them in the fridge. Heat the grill to very hot.
6. Sprinkle the top of each ramekin with demerara sugar, and glaze under the grill. Allow the sugar to set hard, then turn them out on to plates.
7. Serve each crème brûlée surrounded by raspberry coulis, and decorated with 4 raspberry halves.

tiramisù

SERVES 8

This Italian pudding is easy to make, and a good idea when you haven't much time. I sometimes serve it in *tuiles* (tulip baskets), but you can make it in a coffee cup or anything similar. I make my own *biscuits cuillères*, but you can use bought langue de chat biscuits if you like.

1 egg

70 g (2¾ oz) caster sugar

125 g (4½ oz) Mascarpone cheese

120 ml (4 fl oz) double cream

16 biscuits cuillères (Basic 32) or langue de chat biscuits

100 ml (3½ fl oz) espresso coffee

50 ml (2 fl oz) Amaretto

cocoa powder

1. Make the tiramisù cream by whisking the egg and sugar together in a bowl in a bain-marie until it reaches 50°C/122°F. Remove from the bain-marie, and cool the sabayon by whisking firmly.
2. Cream together the Mascarpone and the double cream, and whisk into the cold sabayon until smooth. Set aside.
3. Just before you serve, soak 8 of the biscuits in a mixture of the espresso coffee and Amaretto.
4. Place the cups on individual plates, pour a little tiramisù cream over the bottom of each, put in a soaked biscuit, and then fill the cups with more cream to the rim. Dust with cocoa powder, and serve with the remaining biscuits to dip.

p

vanilla crème brûlée

Chocolate fondant

SERVES 4

This lovely warm chocolate mousse is quick to make.

75 g (3 oz) dark chocolate
75 g (3 oz) unsalted butter
1 egg
1 egg yolk
30 g (1¼ oz) caster sugar
8 g (¼ oz) plain flour

1. Preheat the oven to 180°C/350°F/Gas 4. Melt the chocolate slowly in a bowl over a pan of hot water on the stove, then add the butter and stir until thoroughly mixed.
2. In another bowl, whisk the sugar and eggs together, and mix into the melted chocolate.
3. Gently fold in the sieved flour, then pour the mixture into 4 small moulds. Cook in the oven for 7 minutes, before turning out on to dessert plates.

p

prune and armagnac ice cream

prune and armagnac ice cream

SERVES 6

This is a wonderful combination of flavours, well worth the cost of buying a bottle of Armagnac. The best prunes come from Agen in France and Elvas in Portugal. As for the ice cream, very good brands can be bought – or you can make your own as we do. In any event, for this recipe you will need an ice-cream maker.

about 200 g (8 oz) pitted Agen prunes
enough Armagnac to cover
250 ml (9 fl oz) vanilla ice cream, softened (Basic 33)
fresh mint sprigs to decorate

1. Soak the prunes for a few hours in the Armagnac, then remove and chop finely.
2. Mix 65 ml (2½ fl oz) of Armagnac with the vanilla ice cream, and churn in the ice-cream maker to freeze.
3. To serve, place 2 scoops of ice cream on each plate, surrounded by the remaining prunes and Armagnac, and decorate with sprigs of fresh mint.

Sticky toffee pudding

SERVES 6

150 g (5 oz) dates, pitted and chopped
150 ml (5½ fl oz) water
60 g (2¼ oz) softened unsalted butter
150 g (5 oz) brown sugar
2 eggs
180 g (7 oz) flour
1 teaspoon baking powder

FOR THE SAUCE
100 g (4 oz) caster sugar
100 g (4 oz) unsalted butter
juice of ½ lemon
100 g (4 oz) cream

This makes a great baked-sponge pudding, done in individual moulds (we use foil cups with a 4 cm (1½ in) diameter). The dates are soaked in water and bicarbonate of soda to soften them, and then liquidised to make a coarse purée. You can add a touch of Armagnac if they're still a bit dry.

1. Place the dates and water in a pan and bring to the boil. Cook for 5 minutes, then allow to cool and purée.
2. In a round bowl, mix the butter and the sugar together until creamed. Then add the eggs and the date purée.
3. Sieve the flour and baking powder together, and stir into to the mixture.
4. Preheat the oven to 160°C/320°F/Gas 3. Butter and flour your 6 moulds. Fill each one three-quarters full of the mixture, and place in the preheated oven for about 10 minutes.
5. Put the sugar and butter in a pan and bring to boiling point, whisking continuously, until the mixture starts to caramelise. Keep whisking until it reaches a nut brown colour, take off the heat, add the lemon juice and stir in the cream.
6. Turn out the cooked puddings on to plates, and spoon over the sticky toffee sauce. Serve with a scoop of vanilla ice cream if you like.

You can also make this dish as one large pudding, using a baking tin about 20 cm (8 in) square, buttered. When the pudding comes out of the oven (step 6), leave it to rest for 10 minutes. Then prick the top with a fork and saturate with the caramel sauce. Serve with either vanilla ice cream (Basic 33) or clotted cream as preferred.

p

sticky toffee pudding

rhubarb crumble

rhubarb crumble

SERVES 4

Here is another old English favourite, which I think goes best with *crème anglaise* (custard). Rhubarb is sometimes, in the late winter and early spring, the only fresh home-grown fruit available; and this is the time to serve it. Maincrop rhubarb has a tarter flavour than the early forced kind, and may need more sugar.

300 g (10 oz) plain flour
200 g (8 oz) caster sugar
150 g (5 oz) unsalted butter
2 teaspoons ground cinnamon
900 g (2 lb) rhubarb, trimmed and sliced into 3 cm (1¼ in) pieces
300 g (10 oz) caster sugar

1. Preheat the oven to 200°C/400°F/Gas 6. Mix the flour and sugar together, and then rub in the butter to make a crumbly texture, and add the cinnamon. Sprinkle this crumble on to a baking sheet, and place it in the oven for 15 to 20 minutes, until golden.

2. Place the trimmed rhubarb and sugar in a pan and cook gently on a lowish heat for up to 10 minutes (depending on the thickness and ripeness of the rhubarb). Drain through a colander.

3. To serve individual portions, pour the rhubarb into heat-proof bowls, add a layer of crumble on top, and heat for 5 minutes in the oven. Or put all the mixture in a single oven-proof dish, crumble on top, and heat in the same way. Serve with double cream or *crème anglaise* (Basic 30).

p

bakewell tart

SERVES 4

FOR THE PASTRY
125 g (4½ oz) unsalted butter
125 g (4½ oz) icing sugar
half a vanilla pod, seeds scraped out
zest and juice of ½ lemon
3 medium eggs
375 g (13 oz) plain flour

FOR THE FRANGIPANE FILLING
250 g (9 oz) unsalted butter
250 g (9 oz) caster sugar
4 medium eggs
splash of rum
250 g (9 oz) ground almonds
32 g (1½ oz) plain flour
¼ teaspoon baking powder
4 teaspoons seedless raspberry jam

TO COMPLETE
2 tablespoons apricot jam
2 tablespoons water
fresh mint
thick cream

Another classic English dish, which I have always assumed was invented in Bakewell, Derbyshire. We serve small individual tarts at the Mirabelle, but here is the more traditional single tart, for which you will need a non-stick tart dish measuring 20 cm (8 in) in diameter.

1. Preheat the oven to 170°C/325°F/Gas 3. To make the pastry, cream the butter and sugar with the vanilla, lemon zest and lemon juice. Add the eggs and half of the flour, and mix thoroughly. Then add the remaining flour and mix thoroughly. Wrap the dough in clingfilm, and put in the fridge to rest for 15 or 20 minutes.

2. To make the frangipane filling, beat the butter and sugar together until smooth, pale and light. Beat in the eggs and rum, followed by the ground almonds, flour and baking powder.

3. Take four 9 cm (3½ in) tartlet tins and place them on a tray. Put a little seedless jam in the bottom of each, then fill them with the frangipane mixture. Bake in the oven for 10 to 15 minutes.

4. Make a jam glaze by heating the apricot jam and water in a small pan until it reaches a coating consistency. Brush the Bakewell tarts with the jam glaze as soon as they are out of the oven, decorate each with a little mint, and serve with thick cream (or custard if you prefer – see Basic 30).

p

bakewell tart

tarte tatin

tarte tatin

SERVES 2

I published my recipe for Tarte Tatin of Pears in a previous book, but this is the traditional version with apples. I like English Cox's Orange Pippins, because they are firm and don't break down during cooking, and have a richly aromatic flavour (if not picked too early). For this dish you need a copper pan measuring 15 cm (6 in) in diameter, and 5 cm (2 in) deep. Or you can double everything and produce a tart for 4.

100 g (4 oz) unsalted butter
90 g (3½ oz) caster sugar
a pinch of ground cinnamon
2 apples, peeled, cored and halved
1 cinnamon stick
100 g (4 oz) puff pastry (Basic 28)

1. Preheat the oven to 180°C/350°F/Gas 4. Smooth the butter over the bottom of the pan, and sprinkle the sugar and cinnamon evenly over it. Place the apple halves symmetrically in the pan, with their rounded sides down. Pop the cinnamon stick in the centre.
2. Roll out the puff pastry to a diameter of 18 cm (7½ in), cut neatly round the edge. Lay it over the apples, and tuck it down the sides between the apples and the pan.
3. Place the pan on a medium heat, and watch carefully until the butter and sugar begin to make a light-brown caramel, visible around the edges. This takes a few minutes.
4. Place the pan in the preheated oven and cook for 30 minutes, until the pastry is done.
5. To serve, place the pan on a medium heat until the caramel starts to bubble. Give the pan a shake, and turn out on to a serving plate. Serve with double cream.

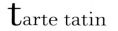

p

pineapple tarte tatin

pineapple tarte tatin

We also serve a pineapple Tarte Tatin at the Mirabelle. You trim and core pineapple slices about 2 cm (³⁄₄ in) thick, and proceed in exactly the same way as for the traditional apple version – but without the cinnamon.

Orange tart

SERVES 8

This is a variation on my lemon tart (see recipe on page 132), and one of my great favourites. We used to serve it at Harvey's in Wandsworth, the first restaurant I opened in London.

250 g (9 oz) plain flour
80 g (3¼ oz) icing sugar
125 g (4½ oz) unsalted butter, diced
grated zest of 1 lemon
grains from 1 vanilla pod
1 egg
50 g (2 oz) sieved icing sugar, to dust
flour, for dusting
butter, for greasing
8 sprigs fresh mint

FOR THE ORANGE FILLING
5 eggs
220 g (8½ oz) caster sugar
zest of 2 oranges
juice of 11 oranges, boiled down to make 300 ml (10½ fl oz)
150 ml (5½ fl oz) double cream

1. Make the flan case as follows. Preheat the oven to 180°C/350°F/Gas 4. Sieve the flour and icing sugar, and work in the butter. Make a well in the flour mixture, and add the lemon zest and vanilla grains. Beat the egg, and add to the well. Knead the mixture with your fingers quickly but very thoroughly until smooth, then wrap in clingfilm and leave to cool in the fridge for at least 30 minutes.

2. Roll out the pastry on a lightly-floured surface to a size just large enough to fill your flan tin, which should be 22 cm (8¾ in) in diameter and 5 cm (2 in) deep, with a removable base.

3. Grease the tin, and fold the dough into it, gently easing it into the corners, and ensuring an overhang of not less than 1 cm (⅓ in).

4. Line the flan with greaseproof paper, and fill with enough dry baking beans or lentils to ensure the sides as well as the base are weighted. Bake in the oven for 10 minutes.

5. Remove the beans and greaseproof paper, and trim the overhang. Return the flan to the oven for a further 10 minutes.

6. Make the orange filling as follows. In a large bowl, whisk the eggs with the sugar and the orange zest. When the mixture is smooth, stir in the orange juice, and then fold in the cream. Continue to whisk until all ingredients are thoroughly amalgamated, and remove any froth from the top.

7. Reduce the oven temperature to 120°C/250°F/Gas ½. Pour the cold filling into the hot pastry (which ensures that the pastry case will be sealed and hold the filling). Bake for 30 to 40 minutes. The middle will still be slightly wobbly.

8. To serve, preheat a very hot grill, sieve the icing sugar over the tart when it comes out of the oven, and then flash briefly under the grill to caramelise the sugar. Cut into 8 slices. Decorate each slice with a sprig of fresh mint, and serve.

p

lemon tart

SERVES 8

The secret of a good lemon tart is that the filling should be firm and clear, and the pastry light and sweet. You can't serve it immediately it is cooked, because the filling will be too runny. Let it rest and set for at least an hour. It will still be warm, and at its best – and it will also taste excellent cold the next day.

500 g (1 lb 1 oz) plain flour
175 g (6½ oz) icing sugar
250 g (8 oz) unsalted butter, diced
grated zest of 1 lemon
grains from 1 vanilla pod
1½ eggs
50g (2 oz) sieved icing sugar, to dust
flour, to dust

FOR THE LEMON FILLING
9 eggs
400 g (14 oz) caster sugar
5 lemons (zest of 2 and juice of all 5)
250 ml (9 fl oz) double cream

1. Make the flan case as follows. Preheat the oven to 180°C/350°F/Gas 4. Sieve the flour and icing sugar, and work in the butter. Make a well in the flour mixture, and add the lemon zest and vanilla grains. Beat the eggs, and add to the well. Knead the mixture with your fingers quickly but very thoroughly until smooth, then wrap in clingfilm and leave to cool in the fridge for at least 30 minutes.

2. Roll out the pastry on a lightly-floured surface to a size just large enough to fill your flan tin, which should be 20 cm (8 in) in diameter and 3.75 cm (1½ in) deep, with a removable base.

3. Grease the tin, and fold the dough into it, gently easing it into the corners, and ensuring an overhang of not less than 1 cm (⅓ in).

4. Line the flan with greaseproof paper, and fill with enough dry baking beans or lentils to ensure the sides as well as the base are weighted. Bake in the oven for 10 minutes.

5. Remove the beans and greaseproof paper, and trim the overhang. Return the flan to the oven for a further 10 minutes.

6. Make the lemon filling as follows. In a large bowl, whisk the eggs with the caster sugar and lemon zest. When the mixture is smooth, stir in the lemon juice, and then fold in the cream. Continue to whisk until all ingredients are thoroughly amalgamated, and remove any froth from the top.

7. Reduce the oven temperature to 120°C/250°F/Gas ½. Pour the cold filling into the hot pastry (which ensures that the pastry case will be sealed and hold the filling). Bake for 30 minutes.

8. To serve, preheat a very hot grill, sieve the icing sugar over the tart when it comes out of the oven, and then flash briefly under the grill to caramelise the sugar. Cut into 8 slices, and decorate with a sprig of mint.

p

b

$\mathcal{B}$ASICS

b

b

Basic 1

Chicken stock

MAKES ABOUT 4.5 LITRES (8 PINTS)

2.75 kg (6 lb) raw chicken carcasses, chopped
about 5.75 litres (10 pints) cold water
3 celery stalks
1 leek
1 large onion
2 carrots
½ a whole head of garlic

1. Place the raw chicken carcasses in a large pot, then cover with cold water. Bring to the boil, then skim.
2. Keep the vegetables whole, but peel them if necessary. Tie the celery and leek together with string – this prevents them breaking up, which helps to clarify the stock.
3. Add the vegetables and garlic to the pot, bring to the boil, skim, and simmer for 4 hours.
4. Pass through a fine sieve. The stock should be a light amber colour, and clear. Store in the fridge for a couple of days, or freeze (but for no longer than 3 months).

Basic 2

Veal stock

MAKES ABOUT 3 LITRES (5¼ PINTS)

8.75 kg (6 lb) veal knuckle bones
120 ml (4 fl oz) olive oil
1 onion, chopped
3 carrots, chopped
3 celery stalks, chopped
½ whole head of garlic
4 tablespoons tomato purée
450 g (1 lb) button mushrooms, thinly sliced
¼ bottle Madeira
10 litres (17½ pints) hot water
1 sprig fresh thyme
1 bay leaf

1. Cook the veal knuckle bones in 4 tablespoons of the oil until golden brown, stirring and turning occasionally.
2. Simultaneously, in a separate pan, cook the onion, carrot, celery and garlic in 2 tablespoons of the oil until golden brown, without burning.
3. Add the tomato purée to the vegetables, stir in and allow to gently and lightly colour. Be careful not to burn at this stage.
4. In a separate pan, colour the button mushrooms in the remaining oil, then deglaze with the Madeira. Boil to reduce down to almost nothing. Add the syrupy mushrooms to the rest of the vegetables.
5. When the veal bones are golden brown, place in a large stock pot and cover with the hot water. Bring to the boil and skim.
6. Add the vegetables and herbs to the bones and bring back to the boil. Skim, then allow to simmer for 8 to 12 hours, topping up the water to keep the bones covered as and when required.
7. Pass through a fine sieve into another, preferably tall, pan and boil to reduce by half. Cool, then store in the fridge for up to a week, or freeze (but for no longer than 3 months).

Basic 3

Veal jus

MAKES ABOUT 1 LITRE (33 FL OZ)

vegetable oil
450 g (1 lb) veal trimmings
2 carrots, chopped
4 sticks celery, chopped
1 onion, chopped
5 tomatoes, chopped
sprig of thyme
bay leaf
330 ml (½ pint) white wine
500 ml (17½ fl oz) chicken stock (Basic 1)
500 ml (17½ fl oz) veal stock (Basic 2)

1. In the vegetable oil, caramelise the veal with the chopped vegetables, add the tomatoes and herbs and cook for a few minutes.
2. Add the wine and reduce by two-thirds.
3. Add both the stocks, and reduce again by half. Season with salt and pepper.

Basic 4

jus rôti

The recipe is the same as for veal jus (Basic 3), but substituting lamb trimmings for veal, olive for vegetable oil, and rosemary for thyme.

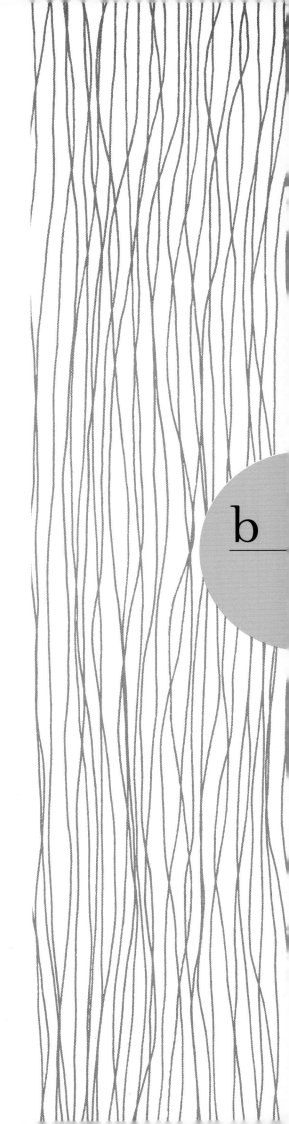

b

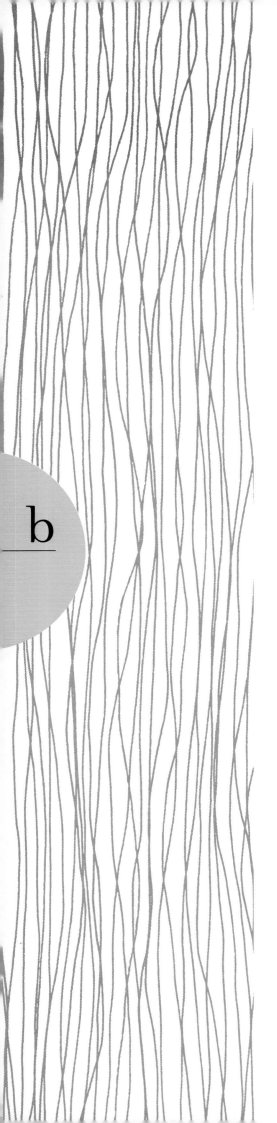

b

Basic 5

fish stock

Makes about 2 litres (3½ pints)

1.8 kg (4 lb) fish bones (turbot or Dover sole are best)
white of 1 small leek, finely chopped
1 large celery stalk, finely chopped
½ onion, finely chopped
½ fennel bulb, finely chopped
½ whole head garlic, sliced horizontally
1 tablespoon olive oil
200 ml (7 fl oz) white wine
2 litres (3½ pints) water
1 lemon, sliced
2 sprigs fresh parsley

1. Wash the fish bones very thoroughly, and chop up.
2. Cook the vegetables and garlic in the oil for a few minutes to soften, without colouring.
3. Add the fish bones and white wine, and cook – without colouring (the bones will turn white) – for about 5 more minutes, then reduce the wine a little.
4. Add the water, bring to the boil and skim well.
5. Add the sliced lemon and parsley, then simmer for 20 minutes.
6. Pass through a sieve and leave to cool. Store in the fridge for a day only, or freeze (but for no longer than a month).

Basic 7

Vegetable stock

MAKES ABOUT 900 ML (1½ PINTS)

2 courgettes
4 onions, peeled
1 fennel bulb
2 leeks
8 garlic cloves, peeled and crushed
14 white peppercorns
50 g (2 oz) unsalted butter
1.2 litres (2 pints) cold water
15 g (½ oz) each of chopped chervil, basil and tarragon

1. Coarsely chop the vegetables. Sweat them in the butter in a large saucepan with the garlic and peppercorns until soft.
2. Add just enough cold water to cover, and bring to the boil. Skim, and simmer for 15 minutes.
3. Add the herbs and cook for another 2 minutes only. Strain immediately. Keep any excess in a covered container in the fridge for a couple of days at most, or freeze.

Basic 6

Court bouillon

MAKES ABOUT 1.75 LITRES (3 PINTS)

3 leeks, coarsely chopped
1 carrot, coarsely chopped
1 celery stalk, coarsely chopped
4 shallots, coarsely chopped
3 onions, coarsely chopped
1 leaf of bulb fennel
a sprig each of fresh thyme and tarragon
a few parsley stalks
1 whole head of garlic, sliced horizontally
1.75 litres (3 pints) cold water
8 white peppercorns
20 g (¾ oz) salt
zest of 1 lemon
1 star anise
250 ml (8 fl oz) dry white wine

1. Place all the vegetables and the herbs in a large pan with the head of garlic. Add enough cold water to cover, and bring to the boil.
2. Add the peppercorns, salt, lemon zest, star anise and white wine, then simmer the mixture for 35 minutes.
3. Pass through a sieve and discard the solids. The court bouillon is now ready to use. Store in the fridge for a day, or freeze (but for no longer than a month).

Basic 8

Sauce vierge

4 PORTIONS

85 ml (3 fl oz) olive oil
25 ml (1 fl oz) lemon juice
1 teaspoon coriander seeds, crushed
8 basil leaves, cut into matchstick strips (julienne)
2 tomatoes, skinned, seeded and diced

1. Warm the oil gently in a small pan, then add the lemon juice and remove from the heat.
2. Add the coriander and basil, and leave to infuse in the warm oil for a few minutes.
3. Add the tomato dice and serve immediately.

b

Basic 9

beurre blanc

1 teaspoon white wine vinegar
2 teaspoons white wine
2 shallots, peeled and very finely chopped
1 teaspoon double cream
250 g (8 oz) hard unsalted butter, diced
salt and freshly ground white pepper

1. Place the vinegar, wine and shallot in a small pan and reduce to a syrup.
2. Add the cream and reduce a little more.
3. Add the butter dice and whisk in until amalgamated. Stir in seasonings to taste, then pass through a fine sieve.

Basic 10

hollandaise sauce

100 ml (3½ fl oz) white wine vinegar
10 white peppercorns, lightly crushed
a few parsley stalks
1 shallot, peeled and chopped
50 ml (2 fl oz) water
1 tablespoon white wine
2 egg yolks
juice of ½ lemon
salt and cayenne pepper
250 g (9 oz) clarified butter, at blood temperature

1. Put the vinegar, peppercorns, parsley stalks and shallot into a suitable pan and boil to reduce by about half.
2. Leave for 24 hours to infuse, then add the water and wine, and strain.
3. Place the egg yolks in a bowl with the lemon juice, and add salt and cayenne pepper to taste. Whisk together, then gradually whisk in the strained vinegar reduction until you have a nice sabayon. The liquid must be added slowly; as it deflates the egg yolks, it strengthens them.
4. After 10 minutes or so of whipping, put the bowl over a bain-marie, and add the butter gradually. Whip until all the butter has been added, and you have a good emulsion. The sauce should be thick and to the ribbon (when the lifted whisk leaves a ribbon-like trail on the surface of the sauce). The sauce can now stand for up to 2 hours if kept in the bowl in a bain-marie, with the water not exceeding 50°C/122°F.

Basic 11

Sauce béarnaise

Béarnaise is the daughter sauce of Hollandaise (Basic 10, above). Add several stalks of tarragon to the vinegar and other ingredients before boiling, reducing and infusing. Make the sauce as above, but add about 25 very finely chopped tarragon leaves to the sauce just before you serve it, not before.

Basic 12

Sauce mousseline

Into each 600 ml (1 pint) of basic Hollandaise Sauce (see page 140), whisk 300 ml (10 fl oz) of semi-whipped double cream.

Basic 13

mary rose sauce

4 PORTIONS

300 ml (10½ fl oz) mayonnaise (Basic 15)
100 ml (3½ fl oz) tomato ketchup
tabasco
salt and pepper

Whisk together all the ingredients until thoroughly mixed.

Basic 14

tomato sauce

4 PORTIONS

40 g (1½ oz) diced carrot
40 g (1½ oz) diced onion
2 garlic cloves, peeled and crushed
25 ml (1 fl oz) goose fat
40 g (1½ oz) plain flour
10 g (¼ oz) Parma ham, chopped
400 g (14 oz) plum tomatoes, skinned, seeded and chopped
salt and freshly ground white pepper
50 g (2 oz) unsalted butter (optional)

1. Soften the carrot, onion and garlic in the goose fat for a few minutes, without colouring, then stir in the flour and cook gently for 15 to 20 minutes.
2. Add the ham and tomatoes to the pan, and bring the mixture to the boil. Add salt and pepper to taste, and cook steadily for 30 minutes, covered.
3. Blend the sauce in a liquidiser, then push through a fine sieve. Don't reboil it, but heat gently, and add the butter if required, to give the sauce a gloss.

Basic 15

mayonnaise

4–6 PORTIONS

2 egg yolks
1 tablespoon Dijon mustard
2 tablespoons white wine vinegar

1 teaspoon salt
a dash of Tabasco sauce
500 ml (17½ fl oz) peanut oil

1. Place the egg yolks, mustard, vinegar, salt and Tabasco in a bowl and mix together
2. Add the oil in drops at first, whisking in so that the yolks can absorb the oil. When about half the oil has been added, it can be added in slightly larger amounts, but continue whisking.
3. Whisk until all the oil has been absorbed and the sauce is thick and creamy. Store in the fridge, covered, for up to a week.

b

Basic 16

bread sauce

400 ml (14 fl oz) milk
1 slice onion
1 clove
4 slices white bread, diced

1. Bring the milk to the boil with the onion and clove. Simmer for 2 minutes.
2. Strain out the onion and clove, add the bread to half the milk, mash together and season. Cover with cling film, and keep warm.

Basic 17

aubergine caviar

AT LEAST 4 GARNISH PORTIONS

1 medium aubergine
1 garlic clove, peeled and sliced
1 sprig each of thyme and rosemary
1 bay leaf
100 ml (3½ fl oz) olive oil
salt and freshly ground black pepper
1 medium tomato, skinned, seeded and finely diced

1. Preheat the oven to 150°C/300°F/Gas 2, and have ready a piece of kitchen foil 60 cm (2 feet) square.
2. Cut the aubergine in half lengthways, and make criss-cross cuts into the flesh with a sharp knife. Into these cuts insert slivers of garlic, the thyme and rosemary leaves, and little pieces of the bay leaf. Place the aubergine on the foil, pour over the olive oil, and season.
3. Wrap loosely but securely in the foil, and bake in the preheated oven for 1 hour.
4. Remove the aubergine from the oven and unwrap it. Scrape the flesh from the skin. Chop very finely with a sharp knife.
5. Add the tomato dice to the aubergine flesh as and when needed. Season if required.

Basic 18

tapenade

8 PORTIONS

250 g (9 oz) good black olives, stoned
50 g (2 oz) anchovies
25 g (1 oz) capers, drained
1½ garlic cloves
2 tablespoons olive oil

1. Place all the ingredients, apart from the olive oil, in a blender for about 5 minutes, and then add the oil.
2. Decant into small clean jars with screw-on lids, and store in the fridge, for up to three months.

Basic 19

pistou

MAKES ABOUT 350 ML (12 FL OZ)

50 g (2 oz) pine kernels
50 g (2 oz) garlic cloves, peeled
50 g (2 oz) Parmesan cheese, finely grated
30 basil leaves
200 ml (7 fl oz) olive oil

1. Liquidise together the pine kernels, garlic and Parmesan.
2. Add the basil and olive oil, and liquidise until smooth.
3. Decant into small clean jars with screw-on lids, and store in the fridge.

b

Basic 20

Vinaigrette

MAKES 400 ML (14 FL OZ)

75 ml (2¾ fl oz) white wine vinegar
salt and freshly ground white pepper
120 ml (4 fl oz) peanut oil
200 ml (7 fl oz) olive oil

1. Place the vinegar in a bowl and add a pinch each of salt and pepper. Stir to dissolve.
2. Add the oils and whisk to an emulsion. Taste and adjust the seasoning if necessary. Store in a suitable container, for up to a week.

Basic 21

boiled potatoes

There are huge numbers of potato varieties on the market, with many different qualities. At the Mirabelle, we use small boiled Jersey Royals for serving with fish, Maris Piper for frying, dauphinois, gratin and rostis, and Desirée for mashed.

To boil potatoes, place them in cold salted water to cover, with two slices of lemon. Bring to the boil, and cook until done – when a sharp knife can be removed without friction.

Basic 22

pomme purée (mashed potatoes)

4 PORTIONS

4 large potatoes
salt and freshly ground white pepper
100 g (4 oz) unsalted butter

1. Peel the potatoes, place in a large saucepan and cover with cold water. Add 1 tablespoon salt, bring to the boil, and simmer until tender.
2. Drain the potatoes, and place in a vegetable mill. Purée, then pass through a fine sieve.
3. Beat in 75 g (3 oz) of the butter, and season to taste. At this stage the purée can be kept aside in the fridge.
4. To serve, warm the purée through in a saucepan, and beat in the remaining butter. Season to taste, and serve.

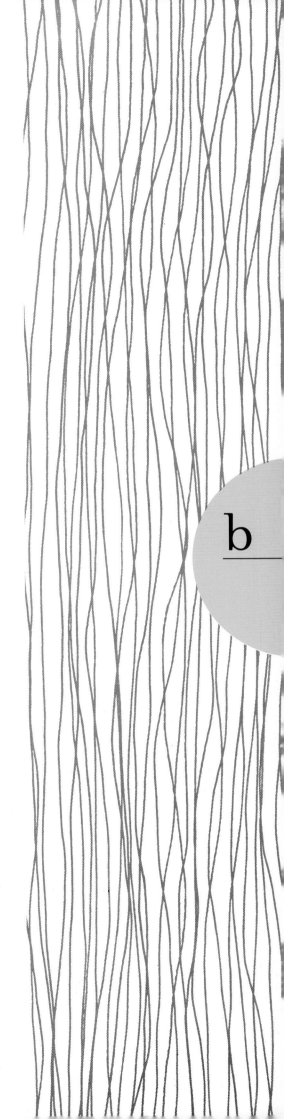

b

Basic 23

pomme fondant

4 PORTIONS

You can make this about an hour in advance, allowing the potato to absorb the butter.

4 medium potatoes
100 g (4 oz) unsalted butter, diced
salt and freshly ground white pepper
50 ml (2 fl oz) water

1. Peel and square off each potato. Using a 5 cm (2 in) plain round cutter, cut an elongated oval out of each potato. Using a potato peeler, round off the sharp edges of each fondant.
2. Use a saucepan with a base diameter of about 15 cm (6 in), so that the fondants can sit comfortably in the bottom. Line the bottom of the pan with the diced butter.
3. Place the fondant potatoes on the butter and season with salt and pepper. Pour the water on to this, and cook on a slow heat for about 15 minutes on either side until the potatoes are golden brown.

Basic 24

pommes frites

4 PORTIONS

6 large Maris Piper potatoes
vegetable or sunflower oil for deep frying

1. Cut the potatoes into equal lengths about 8 mm (⅓ in) square. Blanch them in water with salt and lemon, by bringing them to the boil, then refresh in cold water. Pat them dry with kitchen paper.
2. Heat the oil to 160°C/320°F, and cook the potatoes for 3 minutes, before draining them.
3. Heat the oil to 190°C/375°F, and cook them again until crisp.

Basic 25

Chips

4 PORTIONS

2 large potatoes (a good choice is Maris Piper)
vegetable oil for deep frying

1. Peel the potatoes and slice them on a mandolin. Wash the slices in hot water, then drain and dry them well on kitchen paper.
2. In very hot oil, deep fry them until golden brown. Drain on kitchen paper, and season.

Basic 26

bubble and squeak

4 PORTIONS

300 g (10 oz) pomme purée (Basic 22)
200 g (8 oz) cabbage, shredded and cooked in boiling salted water for 5 minutes
100 g (4 oz) unsalted butter
50 g (2 oz) flour, seasoned
salt and freshly ground pepper

Mix the potato, cabbage and half the butter together and season. Divide evenly and form into 4 balls. Lightly dust with seasoned flour, and pan fry in a non-stick pan in the rest of the butter, for 4 to 5 minutes on each side, pressing down to form a cake. Remove and keep warm before serving.

Basic 28

Puff pastry

MAKES ABOUT 1.1 KG (2½ LB)

450 g (1 lb) strong plain flour, sieved
1 teaspoon salt
450 g (1 lb) unsalted butter, softened slightly
180 ml (6½ fl oz) water
2 teaspoons white wine vinegar

1. Sieve the flour into a circle on your work surface. Make a well in the middle and put into this the salt, 60 g (2¼ oz) of the butter, the water and the vinegar. Mix and knead until the dough is smooth and elastic. Mould the dough into a ball and score a cross with a knife across the top. Cover the dough with a cloth and leave to rest in a cool place for about an hour.

2. On a lightly-floured surface, roll the dough into a sheet about 20 cm (8 in) square, rolling the corners (the tails of the cross) a little more thinly than the centre.

3. Place the remaining butter in a block in the centre of the dough. Bring up the four corners of pastry over the butter to make an envelope.

4. Roll this out into a rectangle about 25 x 15 cm (10 x 6 in) and fold in three. Turn this folded rectangle by 90 degrees. This constitutes a 'turn'.

5. Ensuring the rolling pin is at right angles to the folds, roll out again to a rectangle the same size as before, and fold in three again as before. Again turn the pastry by 90 degrees (in the same direction as before). Two 'turns' have now been completed.

6. Cover the dough and rest in the fridge for an hour.

7. Roll out again twice in a rectangle, fold and turn as in steps 4 and 5. Four 'turns' have now been completed. Rest the dough for another hour in the fridge.

8. Repeat stages 4 and 5 again. Six 'turns' have now been completed. Rest the dough for one more hour in the fridge, and it is ready to use.

Basic 27

Pea purée

6 PORTIONS

1 onion, chopped
a little vegetable oil
small handful mint
500 ml (17½ fl oz) chicken stock (Basic 1)
1 kg (a bit more than 2½ lb) frozen peas
1 teaspoon sugar
1 teaspoon salt

1. Sweat the onion in the oil until softened but not coloured, add a little mint, and stir for a few minutes. Add the boiling chicken stock, bring back to the boil, and add the peas.

2. Bring back to the boil again and cook until the peas are thoroughly done. Strain off and reserve the liquid.

3. Place the peas in a liquidiser and blend, adding the sugar and salt, and a little of the cooking liquid as necessary, to obtain a nice thick consistency. Serve immediately.

If you need to prepare the pea purée in advance, keep it on ice to preserve the green colour. When it's needed, warm it in a pan with some soft butter, adding more of the cooking liquid as required.

b

Basic 29

Sponge

200 g (8 oz) caster sugar
8 eggs
200 g (8 oz) plain flour

1. Preheat the oven to 180°C/350°F/Gas 4. Break the eggs into a bowl and mix with the sugar to make a sabayon. Fold in the sieved flour.
2. Pour the mixture into a suitable flat cake tin and cook in the oven for 12 minutes until done.

Basic 30

Crème anglaise (custard)

ABOUT 10 PORTIONS

6 egg yolks
100 g (4½ oz) caster sugar
500 ml (17½ fl oz) milk

1. Mix the egg yolks and sugar well together in a rounded bowl.
2. Bring the milk to the boil and pour over the egg and sugar mixture. Mix in well, then return to the pan and to the heat.
3. On a very low heat, continue stirring slowly until the mixture thickens enough to coat the back of your spoon. If you want it a little thicker, you can add a teaspoon of Bird's Custard Powder (see the recipe for Sherry Trifle, page 109).
4. Remove from the heat and pass through a fine sieve.

Various flavourings can be added to this basic custard, Armagnac for instance. Or vanilla or cinnamon can be infused with the milk. Never use a whisk when making custard. This adds air, and you end up with a bubbly sauce. Just use a spoon.

Basic 31

raspberry coulis

4 PORTIONS

225 g (8 oz) fresh raspberries
75 g (3 oz) icing sugar

1. Place the raspberries in a bowl and cover with the sugar. Leave for a while for the sugar to begin pulling out the fruit juices.
2. Purée the mixture, then pass through a fine sieve to catch all the seeds. Chill.

Basic 32

biscuits cuillères

20 eggs
500 g (1 lb 1 oz) caster sugar
300 g (10 oz) flour

1. Preheat the oven to 180°C/350°F/Gas 4. Break 10 eggs and 10 yolks into a bowl, and mix with half the sugar until you have a sabayon.
2. In another bowl, beat the remaining 10 egg whites with the rest of the sugar to make a stiff meringue.
3. Fold the meringue into the sabayon, then gently fold in the sieved flour.
4. Cook in a flat baking tin in the oven for 12 minutes.
5. Remove from the oven, sprinkle evenly with caster sugar, and when cold cut into fingers.

Basic 33

Vanilla ice cream

10 PORTIONS

6 egg yolks
120 g (4½ oz) caster sugar
500 ml (17½ fl oz) milk
6 vanilla pods, split (or vanilla essence to taste)
200 ml (7 fl oz) double cream, whipped

1. Mix the egg yolks and sugar together well in a rounded bowl.
2. Put the milk and the vanilla pods and scraped-out seeds in a pan and bring to the boil.
3. Pour the hot liquid over the yolk mixture and mix well.
4. Return the mixture to the pan and to the heat, and cook very slowly, stirring, until the mixture thickens enough to coat the back of your spoon. This, basically, is a highly flavoured crème anglaise.
5. Remove from the heat and pass through a fine sieve into a bowl over ice to cool it down quickly.
6. When cold, whip in the whipped cream. Put in an ice-cream machine and churn until frozen, or freeze in the freezer.

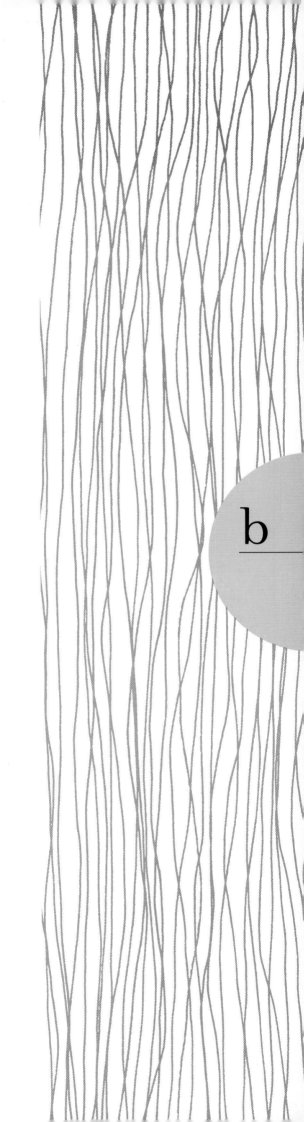

b

MENUS

Les Hors-d'Oeuvre

Les Escargots à la Bourguignonne (½ doz.) 18/6
Les Crevettes d'Algerie (½ doz.) 15/6
Le Caviar de Beluga 35/6
Le Melon de Saison
La Poire d'Avocado (½) 11/6 avec Crabe 14/6
Le Cocktail de Homard 16/6
La Terrine du Chef 10/6
Le Saumon Fumé d'Ecosse 17/6
La Truite Fumée 10/6
Le Jambon de Parme 16/-
Le Crabe Dressé 15/6
Les Harengs Polonaise 16/6
Le Foie Gras de Strasbourg 30/-
Potted Shrimps 8/6
Le Cocktail de Pamplemousse 7/6

Les Potages

La Petite Marmite Henri IV 7/6
La Crème St. Germain 6/6
La Bisque de Homard 8/6
La Tortue Claire au Xérès 8/6
Le Consommé au Choix 7/6
Le Germiny en Tasse 7/6
La Crème à la Reine 6/6
La Soupe à l'Oignon 7/6
Le Minestrone 7/6
La Vichyssoise 6/6

Les Pâtes

Les Spaghettis Bolognaise 11/6
Les Cannelonis au Jus 11/6
Les Gnocchis à la Romaine 11/6
Les Raviolis 11/6

Les Entremets

Les Glaces: Café, Ananas, Citron,
Vanille, Chocolat, Fraise 7/6
La Crème Caramel 7/6   La Pêche Melba 10/6
La Coupe Nesselrode 8/6   Le Mont Blanc 8/6
La Meringue Glacée Chantilly 9/6
La Salade de Fruits 7/6
Le Soufflé au Grand Marnier ou Cointreau
(2 cvts.) 32/6

La Timbale Elysée 14/6
La Bombe Glacée Pralinée 9/6
La Corbeille de Fruits 9/6
Les Petits Fours 3/6

Les Plat

Barszcz
Les Quenelles de
Le Homard Mirabelle   Le Hom
La Sole d'Outre Manche ou Mira
Les Langoustines au Whisky   Les La
L'Omelette Normande ou Arnold Benn
Brioche à la Moëlle   Gratin

Le Medaillon de Boeuf Mirabelle   La C
Le Coq au Vin   Le Poulet d'Estragon
Les Cotelettes d'Agneau Prince de
Le Carré d'Agneau en Croûte
L'Escalope de Veau Farcie
Pojar

Les
L'Ananas Orientale
L'Oranges Orientale
Le Soufflé Arlequi
Le Ga

Les

Le Tournedos Berny 25/
Osso Buco 19/6
Le Foie de Veau à l'Anglaise 2
L'Escalope Viennoise 22/6
La Cervelle au Beurre Noir 18/6
Le Suprême de Poulet Curzon 22/-
Le Feuilleté de Ris de Veau 25/-
L'Escalope de Veau Archiduc 25/6
Les Rognons d'Agneau Duc de Guise
Le Suprême de Volaille Périgourdine
La Côte de Veau Bonne Femme 23/6
Le Kebab à la Grecque 22/6
La Julienne de Veau aux Piments
Les Foies de Volaille au Raisin 2
Le Tournedos Rossini 29/6

Les

Loin Chop Grillé 21/6   Le Filet Grillé 27/6   L'Entrec
Le Chateaubriand (2 cvts.) 52/6   L'Entrecôte Grillé 25

Les

Les Fonds d'Artichauts Florentine 8/6   Les Courgettes Prover
La Bouquetière de Légumes 15/6   Les Haricots Verts Frais 6/6
Le Choufleur au Gratin 6/6   L'Aubergine Farçie 6/6   Le
LES POMMES: Sautées, Nouvelle

Les

Diane 7/6   Croûte Ivanhoe 7/6   Welsh Rarebi

L

Gourmets

vienne
antua ou Brochet
illaise   Le Homard en Brioche
        Les Filets de Sole au Cinzano
au Currie   Le Délice de Langouste
oyarde   Les Oeufs Brouillés Wiltshire
s   Prawns à la Provençale

uf Villette   Le Filet de Boeuf Lucullus
    La Poularde Sautée au Champagne
 Noisettes d'Agneau Edouard VII
 Carré d'Agneau Bonne Femme
ttes de Caneton aux Truffes
ème

ets
ipe Glacé Mirabelle
fflé Glacé Mirabelle
oufflé Rothschild
belle

es
    Le Steak Tartare 22/6
Pochée aux Nouilles 20/6
        Le Boeuf Strogonoff 21/6
Queue de Boeuf Printanière 20/6
    La Timbale de Ris de Veau 23/-
        Le Ris de Veau Maréchale 23/-
        La Tête de Veau Vinaigrette 17/6
a Suprême de Volaille à la Kieff 21/-
        L'Escalope de Veau Nelson 23/6
        Le Ris de Veau Financière 21/6
Le Carré d'Agneau à la Niçoise 23/6
s Crêpes de Volaille Gratinées 19/6
        Le Poulet au Currie 22/6
        L'Entrecôte Bordelaise 26/6
oussin au Beurre d'Isigny 21/-

les
21/-   Le Mix Grill 21/-   Chump Chop Grillé 21/6
Cotelettes d'Agneau Grillées 17/6   Le Rumpsteak 22/6

es
    Les Petits Pois à la Française 6/6   Les Celeris Braisés 6/6
nards en Branches 6/6   Les Artichauts, Sauce Hollandaise 9/6
Vichy 6/6   Les Endives Braisées 6/6   Les Asperges
ites, Soufflées, au Four, Berny 4/6

/
es
cotch Woodcock 7/6   Champignons sur Toast 7/6
6

Les Oeufs

Les Omelettes aux Choix 13/6
Sur le Plat: à la Turque, Berny, Meyerbeer 7/6
Pochés: Otero, Florentine, Bénédictine 7/6
Cocotte: à la Crème, Périgourdine, Chambertin 7/6
Frits: au Vin, Provençale, Milanaise 7/6

⚜ ⚜ ⚜ ⚜

Les Poissons

La Sole Grillée ou Meunière 21/6
Le Tronçon de Turbot Poché ou Grillé 19/6
Truite: Amandine, Vin Rouge, Farcie 18/6
La Truite au Bleu 13/-
Les Paupiettes de Sole Mirabelle 22/6
Le Rouget Grillé ou Niçoise 20/-
Le Loup Grillé au Fenouille 18/6
Le Gratin de Crabe 19/-
Les Sardines Grillées 15/6
Les Crevettes au Currie 19/6
Le Homard à l'Americaine (40 mins.)
Le Homard Cardinal ou Newburg
Les Blanchailles Diablées 12/6
La Goujonnade de Sole à la Crème 19/6
Le Merlan en Colère 12/6
Les Scampi Frits ou Meunière 19/6
Le Saumon Poché ou Grillé
La Truite Saumonée au Champagne

⚜ ⚜ ⚜ ⚜

La Broche et Rôtissoire

Le Poulet de Grain (2 cvts.) 38/-
Le Poussin au Lard 20/6
Le Caneton d'Aylesbury (2 cvts.) 60/-
Le Carré d'Agneau Sarladaise 23/6

⚜ ⚜ ⚜ ⚜

Les Salades

Panachée 6/-   Lorette 6/-
Japonaise 6/6   Orange 6/6
Avocado 8/6

⚜ ⚜ ⚜ ⚜

LE PLATEAU DE FROMAGES 6/6

⚜ ⚜ ⚜ ⚜

Couvert 3/6

Les Plats des Gourmets

Barszcz à la Cracovienne

✤ ✤

Oeufs Brouillés Wiltshire

Omelette Normande ou Arnold Bennett

Omelette Savoyarde

✤ ✤

Croûte de Foie Gras Gratinée

*Quenelles de Homard Nantua ou Brochet

Homard Mirabelle

Homard Deauvillaise

Cassolette de Homard ou Crabe

Sole d'Outre Manche

Sole Mirabelle

Filets de Sole au Cinzano

Scampi au Whisky

Scampi au Currie

Prawns à la Provençale

Gratin de Poissons

Brioche à la Moëlle

✤ ✤

Medaillon de Boeuf Mirabelle

Côte de Boeuf Villette

Filet de Boeuf Lucullus

Côtelettes d'Agneau Prince de Galles

Noisettes d'Agneau Edouard VII

Carré d'Agneau en Croûte

Escalope de Veau Farcie

Coq au Vin

Poulet à l'Estragon (2 cvts.)

Poularde Sautée au Champagne

Pojarski à la Crème

✤ ✤

Trois Sorbets

Ananas Orientale

Orange Orientale

Coupe Glacée Mirabelle

Soufflé Glacé Mirabelle

Soufflé Arlequin

Soufflé Rothschild

Gâteau Mirabelle

Escargots à la Bourguignonne
(1 doz.) £4·30 ✓
Crevettes d'Algerie ✓
(½ doz.) £3·10
Cocktail de Homard ✓
Mayonnaise de Saumon £3·60

Petite Marmite Henri IV £1·00
Crème St. Germain 90p

Spaghetti Bolognaise £1·80

Omelettes aux Choix £1·50

Saumon Grillé ou Poché
*Grenouilles aux
  Fines Herbes £3·20
Sole Grillée ou Meunière £4·50
Tronçon de Turbot Poché ou
  Grillé £4·10
Paupiettes de Sole Mirabelle
  £4·30

Poulet Forestière £4·10
Osso Buco £4·10
Foie de Veau à l'Anglaise £4·00
Escalope Viennoise £3·90
Cervelle au Beurre Noir £2·20
Suprême de Poulet Curzon £3·10
Escalope de Ris de Veau
  Florentine £4·70

Chateaubriand (2 cvts.) £10·00
Poulet de Grain Grillé
  (2 cvts.) £6·50

Poussin au Lard £3·00

Fonds d'Artichauts Florentine
  £1·10
Bouquetière de Légumes £1·65
Choufleur au Gratin 80p

Glaces: Café, Ananas, Citron,
  Vanille, Chocolat, Fraise £1·10
Crème Caramel 90p
Pêche Melba £1·50
Coupe Nesselrode £1·50

Luncheon:
Minimum charge £4·00
Couvert 55p

Les

Royal Caviar de Bel...
  (approx. 1 oz.) £7...
  Melon de Sai...
Poire d'Avocado £1...
  avec Crabe £2...

Tortue Claire au Xérès £1...
Consommé aux Choix ...

Gnocchi à la Romaine £1...

Pochés: Florentine,
  Bénédictine £1...

L...

Gratin de Saumon £3...
Barbue Dugléré £4...
au Fines Herbes £3...
Truite: Amandine, Meunière ...
  £2...
Truite au Bleu £2...
Gratin de Crabe £4...

Entrecôte Grand-Mére £4...
Suprême de Volaille
  Périgourdine £4...
Côte de Veau Bonne Femme
  £4...
Kebab à la Grecque £3...
Sauté de Veau Provençale £3...
Entrecôte au Poivre Vert £5...

L...

Filet Grillé £5...
Loin Chop Grillé £4...
Entrecôte Minute £3...

La B...

Caneton d'Aylesbury (2 cvts.)
  £8...

L...

Courgettes Provençale ...
Haricots Verts ...
Epinards en Branches 8...
Champignons à la Crème £1...

L...

Mont Blanc £1...
Meringue Glacée Chantilly
  £1...
Salade de Fruits £1...

Prices do not in...

Oeuvre

Terrine du Chef £1·20
Saumon Fumé d'Ecosse £5·00
Truite Fumée £2·00
Jambon de Parme £2·40
avec Melon £3·30
Crabe Dressé £3·40

Foie Gras de Strasbourg £7·00
Potted Shrimps £1·00
Cocktail de Pamplemousse 90p
Croquettes de Homard £1·90
Salade Niçoise £1·90
Harengs Polonaise £1·80

...ges

Crème à la Reine 90p
Bisque de Homard £1·20

Soupe à l'Oignon 90p

...es

Ravioli £1·80

...fs

Cocotte: à la Crème,
Périgourdine, Chambertin £1·10

Sur le Plat: Bercy,
à la Turque, £1·20

...ns

Raie au Beurre Noir £3·50
Homard Cardinal ou Newburg
Blanchailles Diablées
Goujonnade de Sole à la Crème
£4·30
Truite Saumonée au
Champagne ou Doria s.g.

Medaillon de Saumon a l'Oseille
£4·50
Scampi Frits ou Meunière £4·50
Crevettes au Currie £3·00
Filets de Sole Marseillaise £4·30
Grand Duc £4·30

...ees

Julienne de Veau aux Piments
£4·00
Rizotto de Foie de Volaille £3·50
Tournedos Rossini £5·00
Steak Tartare £4·00
Boeuf Strogonoff £3·80
Queue de Boeuf Printanière
£3·50

Ris de Veau Maréchale £5·00
Escalope de Veau Nelson £5·00
Ris de Veau Financière £4·50
Fritots de Volaille £3·80
Poulet au Currie £3·00
Entrecôte Bordelaise £4·70
Poussin au Beurre d'Isigny £2·50
*Agneau de Lait Sarladaise s.g.

...ades

Mix Grill £3·80
Chump Chop Grillé £3·80
Entrecôte Grillé £4·40

Cotelettes d'Agneau Grillées
£3·00
Tournedos Grillé £4·70

Rotissoire

Filet de Boeuf Rôti (3 cvts.)
£15·00

Contrefilet Bouquetière (3 cvts.)
£17·00

...mes

Artichauts, Sauce Hollandaise
£1·40
Carottes Vichy 70p
Petits Pois 80p

POMMES
Sautées, Nouvelles, Purée,
Frites, Soufflées, au Four, 80p

...nets

Soufflé au Grand Marnier ou
Cointreau (2 cvts.) £3·80
Crêpe Farci Grand Marnier
£1·60

Crêpe Normande £1·60
Bombe Glacée Pralinée £1·60
Timbale Elysée £1·90

Dinner:
Minimum charge £5·00
Couvert (including Petits Fours) £1·00

...or Value Added Tax

> **The Pine Room**
> This elegant private room
> can accommodate up to 32 guests
> for luncheon or dinner.

Les Salades

Panachée 70p

Lorette 70p

Japonaise 80p

Orange 70p

Caesar Salad (2 cvts.) £3·50

Avocado £1·10

Les Canapés

Diane £1·00

Croûte Ivanhoe £1·00

Welsh Rarebit £1·00

Scotch Woodcock £1·00

Champignons sur Toast £1·00

Plateau de Fromages £1·00

Café 45p

*When available

m

Les Hors-d'Oeuvre Froids

Jambon de Parme avec Mangue ou Melon £7.95
Parma ham with mango or melon

Cocktail de Homard au Cerfeuille £9.50
Lobster cocktail with lime and chervil dressing

Saumon Fumé d'Écosse £10.25
Smoked Scotch salmon

Poire d'Avocat Mirabelle £4.50
Sliced avocado pear with smoked salmon mousse

Tartare de Saumon à la Russe £10.50
Marinated finely chopped salmon with caviar

Royal Caviar de Beluga £21.25
Finest Russian caviar

Mousse de Foie Gras en Brioche £10.00
Mousse of fresh goose liver with pistacchio and truffle in a brioche case

Petite Soufflé de Crabe £7.50
A light crab soufflé

Salade de Caille Fumé £7.50
Smoked quail salad

Les Hors-d'Oeuvre Chauds

Gnocchi Verde £4.50
Gnocchi made with ricotta cheese and spinach

Mousseline de Brochet au Marc de Champagne £8.50
Hot pike mousse in a marc de champagne sauce

Foie Gras Frais Poëlé au Chablis £10.00
Fresh goose liver tossed in butter served with grapes, poached in chablis

Quenelles de Homard à l'Aneth £11.00
Lobster quenelles in a crayfish sauce delicately flavoured with dill

Les Potages

Consommé de Volaille aux Concombres £3.50
Clear chicken soup with chicken quenelles and cucumber

Soupe aux Fruits de la Forêt £3.50
Wild mushroom broth

Tourin de Crevettes Roses £4.50
A soup with pink shrimps and fresh herbs

Crème Cressonière Glacée £3.50
Iced creamed watercress soup

Les Poissons

Sole Mirabelle £13.25
Sole with lobster mousse and scampis in a creamy white wine and chive sauce

Suprème de Saumon aux Ecrevisses £13.25
Fillet of salmon garnished with fresh crayfish tails

Saint Pierre aux Herbes des Provinces £11.25
Grilled John Dory with fresh herbs

Turbotin Poché aux Nouilles Noires £11.25
Poached baby turbot served with fresh black noodles

Fruits de Mer en Matelote £11.25
Fish and shellfish in a mediterranean-style stew

Fricassé de Langoustines Forestière £11.25
Scampis with assorted wild mushrooms

Goujonnade de Sole aux Amandes £10.25
Fine strips of sole with sliced almonds

Cocquille de Crabe au Citron Vert £11.25
White crabmeat tossed in fresh lime butter and served in the shell

Les Entrées

Foie de Veau aux Trois Oignons £10.00
Calfs liver on a bed of spring onions garnished with braised button onions and fried shallots

Aguillette de Caneton aux Abricots £11.50
Sliced breast of pink duckling in an apricot brandy sauce

Rognons de Veau St. Etienne £11.50
Spiced calfs kidneys served with steamed couscous

Coeur de Filet de Boeuf à la Lyonnaise £13.50
Fillets of beef in burgundy wine and served with fresh noodles

Escalope de Ris de Veau aux Points d'Asperges £12.50
Panfried calfs sweetbread with asparagus tips

Steak de Veau aux Baies Roses £10.00
Milk fed loin of veal steak with pink peppercorns

Medaillons de Boeuf Mirabelle £13.50
Fillets of beef in truffle sauce with mushroom tartlettes

Carré d'Agneau Farcie en Croûte £12.50
Stuffed loin of lamb baked in puff pastry with a foie gras and truffle sauce

Les Relevées
Minimum 2 personnes

Filet de Boeuf à l'Essence Raifort £12.50 p.p.
Roast fillet of beef, sweet potato croquettes, braised lettuce with a delicately flavoured horseradish sauce

Canard Rôti à Votre Choix £12.00 p.p.
Roast Aylesbury duckling your favourite way

Poulet de Bresse Rôti au Riz Sauvage £12.50 p.p.
Grain fed chicken from Bresse with wild rice

Gigette d'Agneau au Romarin £10.00 p.p.
Boned leg of lamb roasted with fresh rosemary

Côte de Boeuf Villette £11.50 p.p.
Grilled ribs of beef with a Bordelaise sauce

Les Grillades sur Commande

Ajourd'hui

TUESDAY   24th JULY

notre Chef de Cuisine Stephen Pulman
Vous propose

ESCALOPE DE FOIE DE CANARD A L'ORANGE	£ 4.50
SALADE D'AVOCAT ET CRABE	6.50
GAZPACHO ANDALOUSE	3.50

* * * * *

AGNEAU DE LAIT SARLADAISE	12.50
JULIENNE DE VEAU ZURICHOISE	10.00
DARNE DE SAUMON GRILLE A L'ESTRAGON	11.50
TRUITE SAUMONEE DORIA	11.50

* * * * *

SOUPE AU PAMPLEMOUSSE ROSE	2.95
FRAISES	4.00
FRAMBOISES	5.50
FRAISES DE BOIS	6.00

Les Légumes et Les Salades

Bouquetière de Légumes en Vapeur £2.75   *Assiette de Légumes Tiède Aigre de Champagne* £2.75
Steamed new season vegetables   New season vegetables with champagne
Pommes: Nouvelles ou Soufflées £1.25
Salade de Cinque Feuilles £2.50   *Caesar Salade* £2.75
Mixed leaf salad   Cos lettuce with egg yolk, garlic, anchovies and croûtons

Les Desserts et Les Fromages

Une Carte de Desserts Vous Sera Presentée par Nos Mâitres d'Hôtel
Special dessert menu will be presented to you
Choix de Voiture d'Entremets £2.95   *Plateau de Fromages Affinés* £3.25
Pastries and fruit from the trolley   A selection of cheeses

Cover Charge: Luncheon £1.25 Dinner £1.75 Café £1.25 Cafetière £1.25 Espresso £1.50 Hag £1.25
Minimum charge £20.00

Pre-theatre dinner available between 6.30 and 7.45 p.m.
The elegant new Tapestry Room and the Pine Room are available for your dinner party

**PRICES ARE INCLUSIVE OF
GRATUITIES and VALUE ADDED TAX**

m

Les Hors d'Oeuvres Froids

Foie Gras d'Oie Maison à la Gelée de Vin d'Alsace £14.75

Terrine de Gibier Truffée avec sa Salade des Bois £8.90

Salade d'Artichaut, Crabe et Ecrevisses sur Coulis Acidulé £9.95

Mousseline de la Mer aux Pistils de Safran Sauce à l'Oseille £7.95

Saumon Fumé d'Ecosse £10.75

Huîtres Natives ½ doz. £9.90

Jambon de Parme et Melon £7.90

Crabe Dressé £9.60

❖

Les Hors d'Oeuvres Chauds

Petites Escalopines de Foie Gras au Vinaigre
de Champagne et Muscats £13.80

Trio d'Huîtres Mirabelle £12.50

Feuilleté d'Oeufs de Caille au Fumé de Haddock £7.95

Quenelles de Saumon Fumé à la Crème de Corail £10.25

❖

Les Potages

Bisque de Homard £4.85

Borscht à la Cracovienne £3.75

Consommé de Boeuf au Celeri £3.85

Crème de Fenouil aux Langoustines à l'Aneth £6.50

Soupe à l'Oignon Gratinée £3.80

Les Poissons et les Crustacés

Noix de St Jacques et Langoustines "Sous Cloche" au Parfum
de Gingembre £16.20

Queue de Turbot au Plat Forestière £15.90

Timbale de Fruits de Mer Mirabelle £14.95

Filets de Sole au Caviar Sauce Champagne £16.80

Blanc de Turbot Poêlé à la Möelle au Beurre Rouge £16.50

Cassoulet de Homard Truffé au Beurre de Pistache £26.00

Turbot £16.50   Dover Sole £16.25   Homard d'Ecosse £25.00

Les Entrées

Mignon de Veau à la Crème de Champignons Sauvages £14.85

Tournedos de Boeuf Edward VII £16.80

Feuilletage de Poulet Fermier aux Truffes Sauce Périgourdine £14.10

Filet d'Agneau aux Deux Sauces £14.80

Mignonettes de Chevreuil aux Betteraves "Aigre Doux" £14.90

Côte de Boeuf Villette 2 cvts. £28.00

Toutes les Grillades et Rôtis à la Broche

Poularde de Bresse Truffée au Jus Naturel 2 cvts. £28.00

Filet de Boeuf £14.20   Foie de Veau £11.80   Caneton 2 cvts. £26.00

Entrecôte £14.00   Côtes d'Agneau £12.50   Gibier à Plumes en Saison S.Q.

Les Légumes et les Salades

Panaché Mirabelle £2.50   Salade Verte Melangée £2.75

Légumes du Marché £2.75   Salade d'Endives et Cresson
                                      aux Roquefort £3.60
Bouquetier de Légumes £3.75

Purée de Céleri Rave £2.35   Salade Panaché £2.75

Pommes Soufflées £2.50   Fines au Beurre £2.25   Persillées £1.80

Sautées £1.80   Purée £1.80   Frites £1.80

Plateau de Fromage Fermière £3.75

Les Grands Desserts du Chariot £4.25

Café £1.50   Hag £1.50   Espresso £1.50

Prices are inclusive of Gratuities and Value Added Tax

Cover Charge £1.50   Chef de Cuisine Herbert Berger

MIRABELLE

EGGS BENEDICT - SAUCE HOLLANDAISE 8.50

RISOTTO OF SAFFRON MILANESE 8.50

NATIVE OYSTERS NO. I ($\frac{1}{2}$ DOZEN) 18.00

GASPACHO ANDALOUSE WITH LANGOUSTINES 10.50

BALLOTINE OF WILD SALMON WITH HERBS - SALMON CAVIAR 8.75

FRESH ASPARAGUS - SAUCE MOUSSELINE 10.50

SALAD OF CRAB 'MIRABELLE' - SAUCE MAYONNAISE 12.75

OMELETTE - 'ARNOLD BENNETT' 8.95

BLINIS A LA RUSSE, FROMAGE BLANC WITH CHIVES - SEVRUGA CAVIAR (30g) 40.00

TERRINE OF FOIE GRAS WITH GREEN PEPPERCORNS - EN GELEE DE SAUTERNES 16.95

PARFAIT OF FOIE GRAS EN GELEE - TOASTED POILANE 8.95

SOUPE DE POISSON - SAFFRON ET ROUILLE 8.50

BAYONNE HAM - CELERIAC REMOULADE 10.50

ASPIC OF OYSTERS WITH WATERCRESS - EN GELEE DE CHAMPAGNE 10.50

SMOKED SALMON, PROPERLY GARNISHED - CREAMED HORSERADISH 12.50

TARTE OF ARTICHOKES AND MUSHROOMS - SAUCE BEARNAISE 8.50

SALAD OF YOUNG SPINACH AND WATERCRESS WITH
CRISPY BACON AND OEUF MOLLET 7.50

TARTE TATIN OF ENDIVE AND CARAMELISED SEA SCALLOPS 12.50

FRESH SNAILS A LA BOURGUIGNONE (I DOZEN) 10.75

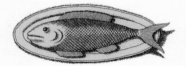

FILLET OF RED MULLET, RATATOUILLE PROVENÇALE - SAUCE TAPENADE 14.50

GRILLED LOBSTER WITH HERBS AND GARLIC, POMMES FRITES - SAUCE BEARNAISE 25.00

CARAMELISED WING OF SKATE WITH WINKLES - JUS A LA PARISIENNE 13.50

ESCALOPE OF TUNA WITH AUBERGINE CAVIAR - SAUCE VIERGE WITH BASIL 14.95

GRILLED DOVER SOLE - SAUCE TARTARE - JERSEY ROYALS, YOUNG SPINACH (SERVED ON THE BONE) 25.00

FILLET OF HALIBUT A L'ANGLAISE - POMMES FRITES - SAUCE MIRABELLE 13.50

FILLET OF SMOKED HADDOCK, POACHED EGG - COLCANNON POTATOES - BEURRE BLANC 13.95

ESCALOPE OF SEA BASS WITH CITRUS FRUITS - CROQUANTE OF FENNEL, FRESH CORIANDER 15.50

ESCALOPE OF COD 'MIRABELLE' - YOUNG LEEKS, BEURRE NOISETTE 13.50

FILLET OF ABERDEEN ANGUS 'AU POIVRE' - POMMES FRITES 16.95

ESCALOPE OF CALF'S LIVER AND BACON - SAUCE DIABLE 14.50

ROAST RACK OF LAMB WITH FRESH HERBS - POMME PUREE, JUS GRAS 18.00

ESCALOPE OF VEAL 'MIRABELLE' - YOUNG SPINACH, FRESH PASTA 15.50

ROAST POULET NOIR A LA VINAIGRETTE - YOUNG LEEKS, POMME ANGLAISE - FRESH HERBS 16.50

MIXED GRILL A L'AMERICAINE 14.50
(LAMB CUTLET, FILLET STEAK, CALF'S LIVER, KIDNEY, CHIPOLATA)

BRAISED PORK CHEEKS WITH SPICES AND FRESH GINGER - ETUVEE OF SPRING VEGETABLES 13.50

GRILLED RIBEYE OF ABERDEEN ANGUS WITH FRESH SNAILS AND GARLIC BUTTER - POMMES FRITES, SAUCE BEARNAISE 15.5

DESSERTS

FRENCH FARMHOUSE CHEESES

CREME BRULEE GRANNY SMITH

FRESH FRUITS IN CHAMPAGNE JELLY,
COULIS OF PASSION FRUIT

LEMON TART

TARTE TATIN OF APPLE WITH CINNAMON

RASPBERRY SOUFFLE (20 MINUTES)

CHOCOLATE FONDANT - BITTER CHOCOLATE SORBET

GLACE NOUGATINE

CREME VANILLE - POACHED FRUITS

ALL AT £7.50

CAFE EXPRESS £1.75

CHATEAU D'YQUEM

WE OFFER A COLLECTION OF FIFTY
DIFFERENT VINTAGES OF CHATEAU D'YQUEM

1990	*350.00	1921	5600.00
1989	325.00	1908	1200.00
1988	460.00	1900	11000.00
1986	*500.00	1895	4000.00
1984	290.00	1894	3150.00
1983	500.00	1893	8000.00
1975	500.00	1892	3500.00
1971	420.00	1891	5500.00
1967	1200.00	1889	5400.00
1962	700.00	1888	8000.00
1961	620.00	1887	4000.00
1959	3500.00	1886	5800.00
1955	1700.00	1884	6500.00
1953	1200.00	1883	4000.00
1947	3500.00	1880	4200.00
1946	1690.00	1877	3200.00
1944	580.00	1872	4200.00
1939	560.00	1871	5800.00
1937	3000.00	1870	15500.00
1933	1500.00	1869	10000.00
1932	1150.00	1867	4500.00
1929	2500.00	1865	10000.00
1928	2600.00	1864	24000.00
1925	1200.00	1863	8000.00
1924	3600.00	1847	30000.00

* Half bottle available - at half the bottle price

SWEET WINES

		GLASS 100ML.	
249	1998 Muscat Beaumes de Venise. Coyeux. France.	5.80	35.00
241	1997 Essencia Orange Muscat. A. Quady. USA. (half only)		20.00
242	1997 Elysium Black Muscat. A. Quady. USA. (half only)		20.00
259	1997 Vendange de Novembre Bourgogne. V. Girardin. France.		49.00
243	1996 I Capitelli Recioto di Soave. Anselmi. Italy. (half only)		27.00
244	1996 Château Les Justices. Sauternes. France. (half only)		39.50
245	1996 Jurançon Noblesse du Temps VT. Domaine Cauhapé. France.	▸	53.00
246	1995 Bouvier Trockenbeerenauslese. Willi Opitz. Austria. (half only)		108.00
247	1995 Tirecul Cuvée Madame. Monbazillac. France. (50 cl)		210.00
248	1995 Opitz One .Trockenbeerenauslese. Willy Opitz. Austria. (half only)		128.00
251	1995 Bonnezeaux, Château de Fesles. France.		71.50
250	1994 De Bortoli Vineyards Noble One. Australia. (half only)	10.00	40.00
252	1990 Côteaux du Layon, Cuvée Anatole Pierre. Domaine Cady. France. (half only)		68.50
253	1990 Château Filhot. Barsac. France.	12.50	85.00
261	1990 Vouvray Château de Gaudrelle. Reserve Personelle. France. (50 cl)		98.00
264	1990 Château de Fargues. Sauternes. France.		125.00
254	1989 Château Rieussec. Sauternes. France.		125.00
255	1989 Château Guiraud. Sauternes. France.	▸	107.00
257	⊕ 1988 Niersteiner Oelberg Eiswein. Gessert. Germany. (half only)		82.50
258	1986 Château de Fargues. Sauternes. France.		132.50
256	1983 Tokaji Oremus. Aszu Essenzia. Hungary. (50 cl)		93.00
263	1982 De Bortoli Vineyards Noble One. Australia.		140.00
260	1975 Rivesaltes Très Vieux. Cuvée Aimé Cazes. France.	12.00	72.50
262	N.V - De Bortoli Vineyards Black Noble. Australia. (half only)		39.00
265	N.V - Moscatel Lustau. Jerez. Spain. (half only)		15.50

INDEX